Birth Fathers and their Adoption Experiences

of related interest

Engaging with Fathers
Practice Issues for Health and Social Care
Brigid Daniel and Julie Taylor
ISBN 1 85302 794 4

Lesbian and Gay Fostering and Adoption
Extraordinary Yet Ordinary
Edited by Stephen Hicks and Janet McDermott
ISBN 1 85302 600 X

The Dynamics of Adoption
Social and Personal Perspectives
Edited by Amal Treacher and Ilan Katz
ISBN 1 85302 782 0

The Adoption Experience
Families Who Give Children a Second Chance
Ann Morris
Adoption UK
Published in association with The Daily Telegraph
ISBN 1 85302 783 9

Experiences of Donor Conception
Parents, Offspring and Donors through the Years
Caroline Lorbach
ISBN 1 84310 122

Child Adoption
A Guidebook for Adoptive Parents and their Advisers
R.A.C. Hoksbergen
ISBN 1 85302 415 5

Birth Fathers and their Adoption Experiences

Gary Clapton

Jessica Kingsley Publishers
London and Philadelphia

First published in the United Kingdom in 2003
by Jessica Kingsley Publishers Ltd
116 Pentonville Road
London N1 9JB, England
and
325 Chestnut Street
Philadelphia, PA 19106, USA

www.jkp.com

Copyright © 2003 Gary Clapton

Library of Congress Cataloging in Publication Data
A CIP catalog record for this book is available from the Library of Congress

British Library Cataloguing in Publication Data
A CIP catalogue record for this book is available from the British Library

ISBN 1 84310 012 6

Printed and Bound in Great Britain by
Athenaeum Press, Gateshead, Tyne and Wear

Contents

ACKNOWLEDGEMENTS   6

Part I Introduction: Adoption and Birth Parents, Birth Fathers and Fatherhood

1   Introduction   11
2   Adoption and Birth Parents: From Out of the Shadows   17
3   Birth Fathers: What Do We Know?   29
4   Fatherhood Today   47

Part II The Life Experiences of Birth Fathers

5   The Birth Fathers, the Pregnancy and the Birth of the Child   63
6   The Adoption   89
7   Life After Adoption   125
8   Birth Father and Child: Towards Meeting and the Meanings of Contact   155

Part III Birth Father Narratives: The Implications

9   Understanding Men and Fathers   191
10   Working with Fathers   201

REFERENCES   213
SUBJECT INDEX   229
AUTHOR INDEX   233

Acknowledgements

My friends and family are due praise and thanks for their patience and forbearance. This especially applies to Lawrie and Jamie. Maggie Mellon's contributions and encouragement have been instrumental. Professor Malcolm Hill is especially thanked for his editorial advice.

To the 30 birth fathers who participated in the study praise and gratitude are due: praise for being honest about matters that are difficult to talk about and gratitude for replying to my appeal and being willing to share such sensitive thoughts and feelings.

Finally, I want to thank Jane. Her contact with me set in motion the ideas for this work. Our continuing relationship is a matter of great importance in my life.

For Jane

Part I

Introduction

Adoption and Birth Parents,
Birth Fathers and Fatherhood

Chapter One

Introduction

Introduction

This book is the first to be written about birth fathers in adoption. It is also intended as a contribution to our knowledge of the place of fatherhood in men's identities. Both of these subjects are a matter of contemporary public interest.

Fathers and their behaviour have never been more under discussion and examination than at present. Lewis describes fathering and fatherhood as having come under 'unprecedented scrutiny' (2000). From 'absent fathers' to government policy initiatives for young dads, from the rights of children born of sperm donors to calls for men to be more involved with their sons, everyone has a view about what fathers should do. Much less is known about what a father is – how men think of themselves as fathers – a central factor in measuring how men should behave. Until much more is known about the emotional and psychological worlds of fathers, decisions that affect the lives of children and their families will continue to be based on stereotypes and false assumptions. The renewed government emphasis upon adoption and consequently the reduction or total severance of links with an increased number of birth parents also make any work on the effects of permanent separation extremely relevant.

The book's origins lie in a mixture of professional and personal interest. In 1994 I met with my daughter whom I had last seen 25 years previously when she was a six-week-old baby, just prior to her adoption. I became aware that our contact was one of many which were and are being sought by adopted people and their birth mothers, fathers or other relatives (Feast 1994). I imagined therefore that I was probably only one of a number of men who sought or who welcomed contact with their biological or 'birth' children and so I searched for reports of others in my situation. However, almost simultaneously, this search developed into what has been as much a professional and academic as a personal journey. I wanted to discover men's motivations for contact. What had moved them to seek or to welcome meeting with and contact from children that they had fathered but not parented? What were their hopes and fears? Before and at meeting, and during any subsequent contact, how did these 'birth fathers' understand their relationship with the adopted child, now an adult? Aside from anecdotal accounts from men in such circumstances I found only two other published pieces of work about birth fathers. This further stimulated my curiosity and my idea for the study came into being.

I set out to interview men involved in meetings with their adopted children. Why had they sought or welcomed contact? The more this question came into focus, the more it seemed to lead to a larger one regarding the nature and our understanding of biological fatherhood and of conventional fatherhood (i.e. being a male parent to a child). Here were men whose only connection with their child appeared to be a biological one. Yet what was their motivation for a meeting with a child they had never parented, a person with whom they had had no social relationship?

A second factor that helped shape the study was a practical one. I soon discovered that there was little sign of men who had been involved in later-life contact with their adopted children. There is (now) much research on women ('birth mothers') who have had their babies adopted. A number of studies have provided examples of biological parents' experiences of adoption and life afterwards, together with evidence of women's desire for and involvement in later-life contacts with their adopted children. However, I found that the adoption experiences of men were missing. The study's scope was therefore necessarily widened to include any man who had had the experience of their child being adopted as a baby – not only the few identifiable birth fathers who had had contact with their children in later life. I felt that this would allow for a comparison with existing birth mother research. Furthermore, the thoughts and feelings of men who saw themselves as fathers but had had no parenting experience, I surmised, might also provide insight in respect of fatherhood in general.

A central question about the place of the child and the adoption in the men's lives then became clearer. What would motivate biological fathers to seek contact with an adopted child? How had they felt about the child at the time of the adoption; in the years since; and for some at least, had there been a change in feeling to make them want to see a child they had originally decided not to parent? What did they want from their unknown son or daughter?

In the course of this work a wider question was raised: that of the differential experiences and expectations of mothers and fathers when separated from their children. Is it 'natural' to expect that women will suffer feelings of loss in relation to an adopted child, but that men will 'naturally' not suffer similarly, nor seek any later-life meeting? There are many untested assumptions regarding men and women and parents as a whole. Such assumptions include that it is 'natural' for a woman to have maternal feelings for the child that has been adopted, and feelings of puzzlement that a man in similar circumstances could feel paternal. Maternity as a biological fact in itself is widely assumed to be inherently associated with maternal feeling, whereas paternity as a biological fact is assumed to be divorced from paternal feeling. Certainly the underlying suggestion might be that whilst men forget about their adopted children, women do not. Previous birth parent research has focused almost exclusively on the mother, in keeping with the general field of social work literature in which the exclusion of fathers from the discussion of children and families is striking. The absence of empirical evidence relating to the feelings, thoughts and behaviour of birth fathers means that this study has broken new ground.

The adoption experiences of the 30 men involved in this study were collected in a series of in-depth interviews, covering the period before the birth of the child, the birth itself, the adoption and immediate post-adoption events. The men's life-long thoughts about their children and the effect of the adoption experience on their subsequent lives were also discussed, as were their motivations for searching for and contact with the adopted child. In the case of ten men, they were able to talk about meeting with their son or daughter in later life. The interviews with the men followed a chronological order starting at the moment they heard news of pregnancy. The narratives that followed went onto the birth and adoption and through until the time of the interview. The presentation of the men's accounts has kept to this framework. Each phase concludes with a discussion of the emergent themes during that period. A benefit of this method of presentation is that it is possible to identify clearly the various points and times of change when professional intervention would have been at its most helpful. Such points and times of change relate to events of over 20 years ago and, as will be discussed, the nature of adoption has changed with many fewer baby adoptions occurring. For such adoptions as still take place the study has direct relevance. For other adoptions (e.g. older children), the men's experiences of giving up a baby that they had not parented may be of less practical professional relevance. However it will be argued that social work attitudes to fathers in adoption may not have altered a great deal. Direct lessons for today's practice emerge again when the study presents information from the more contemporary experiences of the men in this study, involving issues of access to post-adoption services, contact and mediation.

With its insight into the feelings of fathers whose children have been adopted, this book challenges conventional assumptions about fathering, paternity and men's relationships with their children. It will be of direct relevance to those involved in adoptions and working with post-adoption issues and shows that men's absence from the adoption process is not necessarily a matter of choice or an indication of a lack of concern for their child. The growing interest in later-life adoption matters such as adopted persons' sense of identity and contact and reunions between birth parents and their adopted children means that the information and understandings offered in this book will be indispensable. In addition, policy makers and practitioners in the broad field of children and families will find this book useful with its practical examples of how men feel about their children from whom they are apart. The insights gained and issues raised in this book bring an informed voice to the current policy, legislative, professional and media debates on the role of men and fathers.

The wider context of the experiences of the birth fathers in this study has three interlocking aspects and the book begins with a discussion of these. First, adoption policy and practice and the place of birth parents in this; there follows an examination of the little we know about birth fathers. Our understandings about fathers and fatherhood are then reviewed. The next and middle part of the book sets out and discusses the lives of the birth fathers in the study. The conclusion of the book draws together the main themes and discusses their implications.

This study came into being as a result of personal experiences and feelings (what study of human beings and their loves and lives does not?), but through consistency of interview structure, standardised questionnaire and external supervision by Professor Lorraine Waterhouse and Dr Fran Wasoff of the University of Edinburgh it is hoped that any personal bias has been kept to a minimum. I hope that this book is read with the same passion and interest with which it has been written.

Chapter Two

Adoption and Birth Parents: From Out of the Shadows

Adoption Today

The UK Government has expressed a renewed interest in adoption (Department of Health 2000a and 2000b; Performance and Innovation Unit 2000) as a means to secure permanent families for children. In 1999 adoption was described as 'fast becoming one of the major political battlegrounds' of the Government (Hirst 1999 p.22). Since then public engagement with adoption has kept up: 'the national debate about adoption could hardly be more high profile…' (Editorial *Community Care* 27 June 2002). In wider society, adoption stories are never far away from the news and find fictional expression in television soaps, plays and on film (Clapton 1996b). During the winter of 2000–2001 the *EastEnders* storyline of Sonia who was pregnant and faced with the option of having her child adopted was followed by millions in the UK. However, the number of out-of-family adoptions (that is adoptions of children by non-birth family members) has been decreasing since the 1970s.

The peak of all UK adoptions that took place at birth was in 1968. Then, 15 babies in every thousand were adopted by people who were not biologically related to the child (Howe, Sawbridge and Hinings 1992). The year after (1969) saw the peak of all UK non step-parent adoptions when 18 babies per thousand live births were adopted (Grey 1971).

Table 2.1 Adoptions in England and Wales 1963–1992 and all live births				
	All adoptions	*Live births*	*Adoptions of infants under 12 months**	*Adoptions of infants under 12 months by non-parents ('stranger adoptions')***
1963	17,782	854,055	9896	9714
1968	24,831	819,272	12,641	12,408
1973	22,647	675,953	6026	5822
1978	12,121	596,418	2816	2786
1983	9029	629,134	1962	1907
1988	7390	693,577	1235	***
1992	6859	673,467	661	

Source: Registrar General's Statistical Review of England and Wales, OPCS

* The figures in this column represent all adoptions, including those by step-parents.

** Whilst the figures in this column may include adoptions by non-parental relatives such as grandparents, the vast majority consist of out-of-family adoptions.

*** From 1985 onwards the annual figure for non-parental adoptions of infants is not available (OPCS letter, 7 September 1995).

Table 2.2 Adoptions in Scotland 1963–1993 and all live births			
	All adoptions	Live births	Adoptions of infants under 12 months *	Adoptions of infants under 12 months by non-parents ('stranger adoptions') **
1963	1683	102,691	not available	not available
1968	2155	94,786	1332	1318
1973	1900	74,392	925	919
1978	1356	64,295	401	394
1983	1164	65,078	291	288
1988	868	66,212	132	131
1993	805	63,337	72	34

Source: General Register Office for Scotland, Population Statistics Branch

* The figures in this column represent all adoptions including those by step-parents.

** Whilst the figures in this column may include non-parental relatives such as grandparents, the vast majority consist of out-of-family adoptions.

Howe *et al.* (1992) calculate that at a conservative estimate there are a half-million birth mothers in the UK and argue that a figure of 600,000 is more accurate. Tugendhat (1992) puts the figure at three-quarters of a million. In my article (Clapton *op. cit.*) I argue that the numbers of people involved in adoption are considerable. If the adopted person, their birth mother and adoptive parents are included in calculations then the number of people immediately affected are four for every adoption. This figure does not take into account other relatives such as birth and adoptive siblings and birth and adoptive grandparents, nor does it include the birth father. Using the conservative figure of half-million adoptions, if the four key parties in adoption are included, then a suggested figure for those who have, incontestably, a direct experience of adoption would be two million. This is roughly 1 in 25 of the population. Some have put the potential figure for those affected by adoption as high as 1 in 9 (Natural Parents Group 1993) or even 1 in 5 of the population (Talk Adoption 1999). A factor that lends controversy to the subject of adoption and makes it a sensitive issue is that adoption can trigger deeply held beliefs in relation to who should or should not be a parent. Witness the controversy in early 2001 regarding the Kilshaw family and the two babies bought by them over the Internet. The controversial nature of adoption, and the many that are directly touched by it, ensures a societal interest that is rarely far below the surface.

Birth Parents

There is a small but growing body of birth parent research that in practice has been about birth mothers (Bouchier, Lambert and Triseliotis 1991; Deykin, Campbell and Patti 1984; Hughes and Logan 1993; Mander 1995; Winkler and van Keppel 1984). This has shown that the birth parent experience can produce 'profound and protracted grief reactions, depression and an enduring pre-occupation with and worry about the welfare of the child' (Brodzinsky 1990, p.304). Other findings have challenged some of the certainties of previous adoption practice, e.g. that birth mothers can and should put the adoption behind them and get on with their lives (Howe *et al.* 1992; Powell and Warren 1997). The identification of continued parent-like feelings and thoughts amongst birth mothers questions recommendations such as those of Rowe who sharply divided biological parenting from social parenting: 'A differentiation of parenting from the act of giving birth is probably an essential part of genuine acceptance of adoption' (1977, p.92). Seven years after Rowe's remarks, emergent findings from birth mother experiences showed that feeling like a parent is an emotion that cannot be simply shut off (Winkler and van Keppel 1984).

Growing birth parent research has also generated an official move to include a role for birth parents in UK adoption legislation: a Department of Health (DoH) and Welsh Office consultation document acknowledges 'a growing recognition of the need to involve birth parents in the adoption process' (1992, p.2). In 2000 the DoH issued 'Intermediary services for birth relatives: Practice guidelines'. Although not mandatory these guidelines are a recent example of Government acknowledgement of the needs of birth parents.

However the experiences and views of birth parents have been drawn from studies that have dealt with birth mothers only. The DoH guidelines referred to above do not refer to birth fathers. This is an up-to-date example of how the experiences and views of birth fathers have not informed debates and the opinion-forming process. As we shall see, whilst birth mothers have been marginalised (in so far as they could be) in the adoption process, birth fathers remain shadowy figures discounted from all but the most cursory efforts at inclusion.

The Changing Context of Adoption Policy and Practice: Gender, Power and Birth Parents

Men and women have been treated in a gender-specific manner throughout the history of adoption law, policy and practice. Accordingly birth parents will have gendered accounts of their experiences of the adoption process. The following brief discussion helps to set birth parents' research and accounts in an historical context. As a majority of the accounts of birth fathers in this study begin in the 1960s, I have chosen to look at the shifting attitudes and treatment of birth parents that date from about this period.

The attitudes of the 1960s regarding unmarried mothers and fathers (predominantly negative) were little different from those that existed in previous decades (Davidoff *et al.* 1999; Howe *et al.*

1992; Petrie 1998). Whilst the interests and needs of the child and the adoptive parents have tended to come before those of birth parents (Logan 1996; Ryburn 1996; Watson 1986), some noteworthy shifts have occurred in adoption policy and practice regarding the respective positions of birth mothers and birth fathers. I begin with the position of birth mothers.

In the 1950s and 60s the predominant attitude was that of social censure directed towards all unmarried mothers. In postwar society, expectations of women were that they play a role that maintained notions of the nuclear family, with the gender inequalities that this entailed. For instance, women were expected to be mothers, wives and housekeepers and men were designated economic providers (Davidoff *et al.* 1999). Illegitimacy brought forth societal condemnation, prejudice and stigma. In the middle of the so-called 'swinging sixties', Scarman noted that unmarried mothers were '...subjected by society to the black sheep treatment. Sometimes rejected even by their own families, they almost always have difficulty with their neighbours and they lose the normal comforts of society' (1968, p.1).

Women who conceived children 'out of wedlock' were seen as transgressing societal mores and norms. Birth mothers faced social opprobrium because of the illegitimate nature of the pregnancy on top of which there was condemnation arising from their involvement in having their child adopted (Edwards and Williams 2000; Farrar 1997; Petrie 1998; Powell and Warren 1997). Mullender and Kearn remark that 'the attitudes which have prevailed towards women having children outside marriage [are] the attitudes which have also shaped adoption' (1997, p.4). Such attitudes led to cruel practices.

Birth mothers were treated as children (Watson 1986); publicly humiliated by being sent to institutions such as mother and baby homes run by restrictive and morally disapproving regimes (Bouchier *et al.* 1991; Edwards and Williams 2000) or sent to 'aunts' miles away from home and family (Wadia-Ells 1996). The attitudes of many professionals in the health and welfare services reflected societal attitudes towards unmarried mothers and birth mothers in particular. At the point of birth, women whose babies were to be adopted were often advised not to look at their infant (Bouchier *et al.* 1991; Farrar 1997). Baran, Pannor and Sorosky interviewed mental health staff and were told that birth mothers had 'sinned, suffered and deserved to be left alone' (1977, p.58). During this period there were many dedicated staff involved with birth mothers who believed that what they were doing was for the good of the birth mother (Triseliotis 1991). However, the experiences of many birth mothers indicate widespread social censure and even bigotry (Shawyer 1979).

Paradoxically, given such social condemnation and treatment, birth mothers were the centre of attention during the time of the pregnancy and birth (Connolly 1978). However this was often not so much in their own right but as the provider of an adoptable child. Birth mothers have reported that they were treated as the primary client in so far as welfare professionals envisaged the end result being the placement of a baby with a childless and married couple (Platts 1968; Ryburn 1996). Despite being the focus of considerable attention, birth mothers were often vulnerable and helpless (Bouchier *et al.* 1991) and their needs the least considered of all the parties involved in adoption during this period (Howe *et al.* 1992).

In terms of legal rights, birth mothers in adoption – and unmarried mothers in general – held primary rights over their children (Sarre 1996). As sole guardian of the child, the birth mother's certification was (and is) sufficient to register a child's birth; the birth father was and is under no duty to do so (Burghes *et al.* 1997; Scarman 1968). Similarly, the birth mother's consent to adoption was generally sufficient to complete the adoption proceedings (Grey 1971; Ryan 1996). Unmarried birth fathers had no rights in these proceedings. Despite having formal rights birth mothers were often not in a position to make an informed choice. First, the birth mother's position reflected the inequalities of gender and power for women as a whole during this period (Davidoff *et al.* 1999: Wilson 1977). Second, any formal rights were rendered negligible by the disenfranchisement that faced young unwed mothers in the 1960s and 70s. Therefore birth mothers were often not able to exercise their existing legal rights in any way other than to endorse what they perceived to be inevitable: the adoption of their child.

Since the early 1970s there has been a gradual shift in adoption policy and practice in keeping with changing social attitudes to 'out of wedlock' pregnancies (Logan 1996; Powell and Warren 1997). As wider options have been made available to pregnant women (e.g. increased financial and other support to unmarried parents and abortion), social stigma and pressures have lessened (Davidoff *et al.* 1999). The result of these changes has been fewer babies available for adoption (Shaw and Hill 1998). Adoption policy and practice changed (perhaps as a result of this) and more openness in post-adoption contact and greater birth parent choice in identification of prospective adoptive parents have grown (Baran and Pannor 1990; Wadia-Ells 1996). Contributions to the changing status of birth mothers have also included greater first-hand knowledge of birth mothers' experiences and views (Powell and Warren 1997). However, despite these major shifts, it remains the case that attitudes toward birth mothers have not become universally positive or sympathetic (Logan 1996).

Notwithstanding any positive shifts in attitudes that have taken place toward birth mothers, the same is not the case for birth fathers. Attitudes toward birth fathers have not, until very recently, altered significantly in the UK (although there have been more significant developments in the USA – see below). As is the case in respect of attitudes towards birth mothers that mirror societal opinions relating to unmarried women who become pregnant, it appears that wider attitudes toward unmarried fathers are contained in views about birth fathers (Mason 1995).

In the historical context of adoption policy and practice, birth fathers have either been given little attention or have been the subject of negative professional views:

> ... we offer to the child, a choice of two images of his father – both of which are sadly inadequate. The first, coming from limited knowledge and understanding of him, and often accompanied by silence or embarrassment, suggests that there is something very wrong with this parent – the fact that much is known about the mother and little about the father would seem to indicate that she took responsibility whereas he shunned it, that the mother was the victim and the father the villain. This, albeit negative image, is at least, an image. The second choice is no image at all. It sometimes appears that we have actually been guilty of contributing to a myth that suggests that a child born out of wedlock has only one natural parent. (Anglim 1965, p.340)

Similar observations have followed down through the decades. Platts (1968), Connolly (1978), Watson (1986) and Menard (1997) all echo previous observations on the absence of the birth father from the adoption process. Some adoption professionals held 'the strongest negative opinions' about fathers (Cole and Donley 1990, p.285) and gave 'short shrift to involvement with the birth father' (Schechter and Bertocci 1990, p.63). Baran and Pannor argue that 'Professionals failed to consider the birthfather as having any rights whatsoever. In fact, the birthfather was seen as an intruder...' (1990, p.324). March refers to a 'neglect' of birth fathers (1995, p.110) and Deykin *et al.* note a 'negative attitude held by some adoption agencies' (1988, p.241). On the other hand, there is also evidence of sensitive adoption practice with birth fathers: Sarre notes that 'paternal origins are more frequently recorded than in the past' (1996, p.45).

Irrespective of any policy and practice changes, the birth father in UK adoption legislation has no legal standing (Burghes *et al.* 1997). In the USA, birth fathers have been gradually accorded greater rights since the early 1970s (Doherty 1997);

however, definitions of these rights vary between states and Supreme Court decisions have generally involved issues in respect of the adoption of older children (Menard 1997). In the UK there is now growing acknowledgement of the need for changes in legislation in respect of unmarried fathers (Bradshaw *et al.* 1999; Burgess and Ruxton 1996). For instance, discussions have included the possibility of extending automatic parental responsibility to those unmarried fathers that jointly register the child's birth with the mother (Sarre 1996). However, it still remains the case in respect of key decisions such as consent to adoption that the birth father's present position in law is not on the same footing as that of the birth mother. Whilst there is a trend for UK courts to equate the position of unmarried fathers with that of married fathers, it remains the case that 'it may be a matter of chance whether the unmarried father of a child whose mother does not want to continue as a carer has the opportunity to intervene' (Pickford 1992, p.140). In 2001 the UK Government announced proposals to change this so that unmarried fathers who sign the birth register would be accorded equal rights with the mother (*Community Care*, 29 March 2001).

However neither birth mother nor birth father felt that they had power in the circumstances of adoption 30 or 40 years ago. The birth mother had a central position yet her needs did not. Additionally, although she had legal power, invariably the birth mother felt that she was presented with only one option: adoption. The birth father was rarely involved at all because of attitudes that either saw his participation as irrelevant to the adoption proceedings or regarded him in a negative light. On paper then birth mothers have historically been accorded more power than birth fathers. A closer examination suggests that the power accorded birth mothers has been empty in practice and conferred as a result of the centrality of birth mothers' biological position in the adoption process. Thus adoption policy and practice has reflected wider societal roles for women that are based upon biology rather than social equity. The fact that birth fathers – in the eyes of the law – remain without a locus in adoption would suggest that today we are still guilty of contributing to the myth of the adopted child having only one natural parent.

But does the minor status accorded to birth fathers in adoption have a basis in fact? If not, then what part may prejudice play in the lack of inclusion of birth fathers? To address these questions it is necessary to establish what we already know about birth fathers and the wider subject of fatherhood.

Chapter Three

Birth Fathers:
What Do We Know?

Birth Fathers

There is little research on the less active, non-social dimensions of fatherhood such as the place of their child in the minds of men and their self-perception of fatherhood. This also applies to issues such as expectant fatherhood. Existing knowledge and understandings are varied. Perspectives on fatherhood range from it beginning at birth when social, active fathering commences, to others that suggest unique male psychological changes and the development of feelings of a bond with the unborn child that may commence pre-birth. If fatherhood can develop before birth in the absence of physical and social contact, then what would happen to these feelings when the baby is relinquished for adoption? The circumstances and experiences of birth fathers in adoption offer a unique natural 'laboratory' in which to explore a relatively unresearched dimension of fatherhood – men's consciousness of fatherhood and connection to their child. Yet studies of birth fathers and their experiences are virtually non-existent. Thoburn repeats a 30-year-old call for a study of the views and experiences of birth fathers (Brinich 1990; National Association of Mental Health 1960) when she asks

'What are the reactions of biological fathers of adopted children?' (1992, p.168). Adoption professionals echo this. Bouchier *et al.* call attention to 'the neglected perspective of birth fathers' (1991, p.16) and Speirs and Paterson ask 'If adoption is a "life-long process" for the birth mother what does it mean for the birth father?'(1994, p.37). The missing birth father experience and perspective has been noted elsewhere in debates on openness in adoption (McCroy 1991, pp.82–84).

On the face of it, the notion that there might be a birth *father* experience is at one and the same time obvious (after all it takes two to make a baby), and not so obvious. It is women who become pregnant, carry the child and go through the physical experience of childbirth. Birth fathers cannot 'give up' a baby in a physical or biological sense of the phrase. Men do not carry a baby for nine months; their bodies do not change. So what may be the place of birth fathers in adoption?

In the circumstances of conception, the difference between men and women is that whilst both share a biological and genetic contribution to the child, women have the added developmental dimension of pregnancy and parturition. It is popularly assumed that men's connection to the child begins and ends with the physical participation in conception, if not followed by assumption of the social role of father. A few voices from the research community have questioned such a popular assumption:

> Although a principal protagonist in the existence of the adopted child, the birth father is often viewed as an illusory entity whose only link with the child is his involvement in the biological event. (Sachdev 1991, p.131)

Brinich suggests that negative stereotypes may be at work in relation to how birth fathers are viewed. She calls for a study of birth fathers from a psycho-analytical perspective and goes on to disagree with what she believes is 'stereotypical' in the view that, whilst motherhood is achieved during pregnancy, fatherhood is gained with the act of socially parenting a child (1990, p.59).

Brinich's comment highlights an important question: how do adoption and the adoptive process serve to delineate the various categories that apply to fathers?

Adoption, Fathers and Fatherhood

The nature of adoption divides two, normally co-existent, categories for men. These are *biological* fatherhood and *social* fatherhood. Social fatherhood is here understood as that role played by a male parent that includes knowledge of and interaction with their child. Our knowledge of and some of the controversies that surround social fatherhood are explored in a following chapter. Biological fatherhood is perhaps more easily understood and is here defined as the male genetic contribution to a child's conception – the classic and dictionary definition of fathering – similarly explored later. Conventional fatherhood in this sense combines both the biological dimension and the role of male parent. For a man who is aware of his birth fatherhood, adoption of his child represents an interrupted or suspended convention. The birth parent research, concentrated as it has been on women's experiences (Harper 1993; March 1995), has not included any substantial reference to the father of the child that was adopted. So where might such a father feature in the process of pregnancy, childbirth and adoption? These questions are illustrated in Figure 3.1.

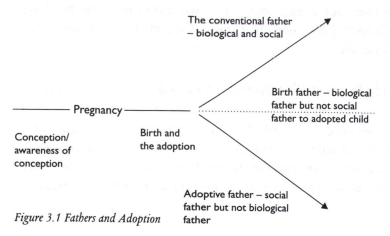

The conventional father
– biological and social

Birth father – biological father but not social father to adopted child

———— Pregnancy ————

Conception/ awareness of conception

Birth and the adoption

Adoptive father – social father but not biological father

Figure 3.1 Fathers and Adoption

The bifurcation depicted here in a conventional father life course – with adoption producing separate birth father and adoptive father narratives – has similarities with a division that may exist in situations where conventional fathers become non-resident fathers and social contact with the child alters (is either maintained or lost). The case of fathers in the latter category – who are fathers without children – has some similarities with the position of birth fathers in adoption. Thus the contemporary relevance of studying fathers without children. In this study the men's experiences and perceptions of themselves may inform the discussion concerning fathers in a variety of situations in which fathers have no contact with their children. Overall the diagram shows how little we know of fathers e.g. the before and after adoption experiences of *adoptive* fathers have also rarely been discussed and, as we shall see, we know little of the pre-birth experiences and psychology of the conventional father.

Previous Birth Father Studies

Thoburn's extensive literature survey for the Department of Health and Welsh Office (1992) is a key source of references on the subject of adoption yet her work is only able to cite one piece of research on birth fathers (Deykin, Patti and Ryan 1988). The study by Deykin *et al.* took place in North America and deals with immediate post-adoptive experiences and the birth fathers' subsequent adjustment. My own extensive inquires have discovered only one other study (Cicchini 1993) carried out in Australia.

The Impact of Child Surrender: the North American Study 1988

Deykin, Patti and Ryan looked at the immediate post-adoptive experience and birth fathers' subsequent adjustment. One hundred and twenty five birth fathers were interviewed by means of a postal questionnaire. An important reservation is made when they point out that the birth fathers in their study were contacted through birth parent support and advocacy groups and note that membership of these groups 'may be motivated by continued concern and distress over the adoption' (1988, p.247). Many of the men were members or supporters of a campaigning organisation Concerned United Birthparents (CUB) which has subsequently been described as 'anti-adoption' (Gould 1995, p.288). The research limitations produced by this reliance upon CUB have been noted elsewhere (Brinich 1990). It remains the case, however, that obtaining data for research in the field of post-adoption experiences depends upon the 'visibility' and self-selection of those who have indicated a wish to be in touch with their adopted children or who (in the case of adopted people) contact their birth parents (Triseliotis 1991). Those birth parents and adopted people who do not seek contact or are not involved with post-adoption services, e.g. counselling, are generally much harder to contact.[1] The findings of Deykin *et al.* focused on attitudes to the adoption, involvement in the adoption process, effects on subsequent marital functioning, procreation and parenting. It was found that those fathers who were in favour of adoption and felt unprepared for fatherhood were involved in the adoption proceedings whereas those who were opposed to the adoption and felt coerced by outside pressures were likely to be excluded. On the questions of subsequent marital functioning and parenting, having been a birth father seemed not to affect marital relations. Few birth fathers reported that the adoption experience had had any impact on their subsequent parenting function.

A central finding was that a 'desire to search' was a common feeling. It was found that, even after extended periods of time, the surrender of a child for adoption remained a conflict-ridden issue

---

1 Recent UK research (Howe and Feast 2000) has achieved a study comparison by identifying adopted people who search and those who do not. This involved the close co-operation of a major adoption agency and consideration of ethical issues such as locating and contacting adopted people, many of whom had previously shown no curiosity as to their birth origins or adoptive status.

for the men. The researchers also found, however, that search activity was highly associated with serious thoughts of taking the child back (1988, p.244). This contrasted with the feelings of birth mothers in a previous study (Deykin, Campbell and Patti 1984) in which it was found that birth mothers' search motivations stemmed from a need to 'alleviate guilt and restore self-esteem through the assurance that the child was alive and well' (1988, p.248). The 'taking back' motivation in the birth fathers' reasons for searching for the child was seen to be a gender difference of possible significance and as such has been repeated subsequently (Mullender and Kearn 1997; Rosenberg 1992).

The research did not explore pre-adoptive experiences (reaction to pregnancy, involvement or otherwise in birth events) or subsequent contact and or reunion between the men and their children. Neither did it address any of the men's thoughts and feelings, unlike the second existing study of birth fathers.

The Development of Responsibility: the Australian Study 1993

In 1993 a paper was published on a more in-depth study of birth fathers (Cicchini 1993). Cicchini argues that the North American study was limited in its ability to shed light on birth fathers' emotional experiences and concerns. Also singled out for criticism was a key conclusion of the previous study: that the search activity of birth fathers was highly associated with thoughts of taking the child back. This, it is argued, was a flawed conclusion because the North American study included only one question regarding feelings – those of responsibility towards the child. Cicchini set out to redress this in his study by exploring the emotions and thoughts of birth fathers 'to clarify motivations behind the search' (1993, p.5). The findings are worth discussing in some detail because they represent the first insight into not only the behaviour of birth fathers but also their thoughts and emotions.

Thirty men were interviewed after a series of appeals in the local and national media. In this respect the Australian birth fathers were not perhaps as liable to exhibit bias as those who had been recruited via birth parent support and interest groups. A large majority of the men in the Australian study had experiences of both the pregnancy and adoption. A majority had minimal or no say in the adoption and in relation to this, their feelings of exclusion were strong. A large majority (83%) did not see or touch the baby but a majority (60%) said they would have liked more contact with the baby. In the weeks and months immediately after the birth and adoption, many reported thinking about the child frequently. The adoption experience was described as 'a period of crisis, emotionally disturbing, marked by feelings of confusion and ambivalence... Only one or two felt no strong feelings' (p.11). Long term, the adoption was 'a most distressing experience' (p.13). Over three-quarters of the men endorsed the statement: 'There is part of me missing'. Five men said that they felt 'positive' about the relinquishment of their child. Twenty-three men had taken active steps to search for the child. Nearly all of the men in this latter group said the reason for searching was to 'ease my mind my child is ok'. Most of those who were searching did so because they wanted to know what the child looked like. For others it was 'to include the child in my life' in the hope of having 'a relationship with my child'. Only a small number were able to report on the effects of contact.

Cicchini found that, in relation to the adopted child, the birth fathers in his study had retained an emotional and psychological feeling of responsibility despite relinquishment of legal responsibility. He concluded that:

> The most significant finding is that the relinquishment experience does not end at the time of adoption, but has enduring effects throughout life... These effects emerge most clearly decades later in a desire to be re-united with the child and seek assurance that the child is alright. (1993, p.18)

There was no evidence of wanting to physically reclaim the child. The Australian work was innovatory because it was the first research to explore the emotional and psychological aspects of birth fathers' experiences. There is much in this work that parallels the emotional and psychological experiences of birth mothers, e.g. the persistence of feelings of distress and loss and the disturbing emotional short-term effects of the adoption.

Out of the Shadows: Birth Fathers' Stories 1995

Out of the Shadows is a collection of 'birth fathers' stories' (Mason 1995); a valuable portrayal and discussion of men's accounts of the effects of separation from their children. However, the collection is methodologically limited because Mason presents 17 stories from too diverse a group. The publication is made up of accounts from men whose broad similarity with each other is their separation from their sons and daughters, under half of whom had been adopted at birth (i.e. more than half had some experience of bringing up their child). There is an overlap between the experiences of men who have become estranged from their children because of divorce and separation (and there-fore have had some experience of parenting) and the thoughts of men who have had no contact with their child as a result of adoption. This makes it difficult to draw any conclusions about the unique position of birth fathers in adoption.

Despite its drawbacks, Mason's collection provides examples of enduring care for the child, grieving over its loss, shame, guilt and damage to self-esteem. One of the birth fathers in the book describes the year of his daughter's birth and adoption as one in which: 'I felt I lost membership in the human race by giving away my own flesh and blood' (p.16). Mason reports damage to self-esteem and, what is to date unique in the research on birth parents, that amnesia about the pregnancy and birth, birth dates, etc. is common among birth fathers.

Even if Mason's study is included it means that there are only three such publications that deal with the experiences of birth fathers. In that case what of any non-research based literature on birth fathers? There is more of this type of material.

Birth Fathers Elsewhere: Individual Accounts and Comments

Individual and anecdotal accounts regarding birth fathers have appeared over the years (Argent 1988; Clapton 1996a; Coleman and Jenkins 1998; Coles 1998, 2000; Concerned United Birthparents 1983; Feast 1994; Hilpern 1998; NORCAP 1998; Pannor, Massarik and Evans 1971; Silber and Speedlin 1983; Tugendhat 1992; Wells 1993a). In these accounts the effects of the adoption are said to have been long lasting and provide back up for the existing research studies. What also emerges is that somehow thoughts of the child have lived on in the minds of these men. One man's account of his immediate post-adoption feelings typifies many of the others: 'How quickly that relief passed and was displaced by occasional totally unexpected flashes from the sub-conscious – a mixture of guilt, curiosity, the certainty of something missing' (Argent 1988, p.19). Argent is typical of many writers who quote birth fathers, speculate that they may well have similar feelings to those of birth mothers and call for research (Mullender and Kearn 1997).

Sachdev (1991) reports on how birth fathers are perceived by other parties in the adoption process. In his study, the attitudes of birth mothers varies from animosity to grudging acceptance (in the best interests of the adopted child) of the importance of information about the birth father. Of all three parties – adopted children, birth mothers and adoptive parents – the adopted children were the most positive in their regard for information sharing with their birth fathers and adoptive parents were the most negative in their attitudes toward birth fathers.

Evidence of adopted children's attitudes towards their birth fathers exists elsewhere (Feast 1994; March 1995; Post-Adoption Social Workers Group 1987; Tabak, 1990). This is not always positive:

> I find it difficult to understand the need of those who seek to know their immediate male progenitor or what they hope to gain from meeting him. I avoid writing 'father' since a father is

> that male person who loves and protects the children in his
> family, whether or not they are genetically related to him.
> Calling a man who just happened to be around at the time of
> conception 'father' is as nonsensical as calling a bottle 'mother'.
> (*The Guardian*, 11 May 1995)

However *Diary of a Reunion* records the thoughts of one woman
which describe a major motivation for tracing both birth parents:

> I watched a programme on adoption, one of the adopted
> children who had found her birth mother said that now she felt
> a complete person – before she had found her mother, a part of
> her had been missing – but how can she feel whole until she has
> found her father? (Feast 1994, p.137–138)

One study of adopted people and birth mother relationships
found that adopted people appear to express 'little interest in the
birth father when they begin to search' (March 1995, p.110).
However this lack of interest is replaced with a desire for contact
with him during the search and after contact with the birth
mother (*ibid.*). Twenty-two people in the study had met with their
birth father (p.118). Types of contact ranged from two who had
felt rejected by their birth father, to two that classified their relationship as 'father-child'. A majority of seven considered the
contact to be 'between friends' (*ibid.*). March found that the
'adoptees' descriptions of adoptee-birth father interaction and
outcome of contact resemble the accounts given for contact with
the birth mother' (p.120).

It seems from adopted people's accounts of searching and
contact that many adopted people have an interest in the birth
father. This is reflected in an increase in anecdotal accounts of
birth fathers' experiences. Yet as we shall now see this interest is
not universally held or echoed by professionals.

Attitudes to Birth Fathers – Professional and Academic Voices

For 40 years many researchers and professionals have called for more information on birth fathers. Also I have already noted negative historical attitudes that class the birth father as either irrelevant or an intruder (Baran and Pannor 1990; Deykin *et al.* 1988). What of more recent attitudes to birth fathers?

In a chapter entitled 'The Birth Father', Tugendhat (1992) quotes a leading UK post-adoption counsellor who wonders whether 'adoptees see him (the birth father) as of less importance?' and asks 'Is he less responsible?' (p.25). Because the questions are not answered, the impression is that they are rhetorical. Tugendhat then states a 'sensible presumption that birth fathers' present families would know nothing of the adoption' and 'so it was better to let sleeping dogs lie' (p.25). However, there is no research evidence for this assumption and whilst there is evidence that the birth mother may be first to be sought out, this does not represent a fixed hierarchy of importance on the part of the adopted person (March 1995; Pacheo and Eme 1993). Tugendhat continues by commenting: 'Men can get away with denying pregnancy and often do' (p.25). A second public figure in post-adoption circles is then quoted:

> Lifton describes her birth father as the type who used to be called a bounder or a cad: 'I see my macho father and his type in the chimpanzee male, who, having had his sport, is off to other parts of the forest'. (p.25)

There follows an account of a US serviceman who had fathered a number of children throughout Europe. Tugendhat remarks: 'This is a perfect example of Lifton's "macho" father who had misspent his youth indiscriminately spreading his seed around' (p.26). In the reports from three adopted people's meetings with their birth fathers that follow, the birth fathers receive the overture to a meeting with resignation 'as if they were waiting for their numbers to come up' (*ibid.*).

Tugendhat's chapter on 'The Birth Father' therefore contains 'sleeping dogs', 'getting away with it', chimpanzees, and promiscuous males who feel consternation that their past will catch up with them. The positive account of a birth father's search and contact with his daughter at the end of the chapter does not redress what, it is suggested, is an overall imbalance in the chapter. Such an absence of balance is disappointing given the lack of birth father research to confirm or challenge such forthright opinions. There is no similar treatment of birth mothers in the literature.

Possible stereotyping of birth fathers is also present in Brodzinsky's otherwise useful review of the literature on birth mothers:

> Historically, the biological father of an adopted child, the 'birthfather', has played little role in the decision-making surrounding the child's birth and subsequent placement in an adoptive home. However, since the 1972 Supreme Court decision in *Stanley v. Illinois*, where a birthfather's legal claim to a child was recognised as protected by the Constitution, considerable interest has been generated in the feelings and legal rights of these individuals... Despite the current move toward increased sensitivity to the rights and interests of the biological fathers of adopted children, it is this author's view that interested, committed birthfathers remain in the minority, with most individuals who father a child outside the protection of marriage, continuing in the centuries-old tradition of abdication of responsibility. (1990, p.315)

The use of quotes around the word 'birthfather' when the same is not applied to the birth mother elsewhere, the phrase 'these individuals', the conflation of birth fathers in adoption with men who irresponsibly father children and the explicit value position on marriage, all convey a general air of disapproval. The one non-contentious opinion is that interested, committed birth fathers appear to be in the minority.

Whether my interpretation of a possible bias in Tugendhat (1992) and Brodzinsky (1990) betrays an over-sensitivity on my part (after all many men do 'abdicate responsibility'), or shows continuing negative attitudes toward birth fathers, is perhaps a matter for a more systematic critique of the adoption literature. However, negative attitudes towards birth fathers may not have entirely disappeared from contemporary adoption literature. This subject is revisited in the conclusion.

March points out what may be seen as the obvious when she talks of 'the saliency of the birth mother's position in the adoption process' (1995, p.34). However, any discussion of the relative experiences of birth mothers and birth fathers perhaps needs to bear in mind that, whilst acknowledging the fact of the birth mother's central part, there may be some drawbacks to the focus having always been on the birth mother (Harper 1993). A question then is whether the marginalisation of birth fathers is simply a result of the birth mother's central part in the adoption process. On the other hand might there be something within adoption discourses that minimises the potential role of birth fathers? The genesis and persistence of such attitudes in adoption theory and practice may have roots in theories of the primary importance of maternal bonding and attachment that have heavily influenced thinking and decision-making in social work in the 1950s and 60s. Arguably, this influence reached well into the 1970s and 80s and may still be present (Daniel and Taylor 1999).

If bias is present in professional attitudes toward birth fathers, a second feature of writings on birth parents is what can be called a conflation. Although the research commonly refers to birth *parents*, it is actually based upon birth mother experiences and views because of the lack of research on birth fathers. In general it is more typically the experience of women that has been invisible to social researchers and the experiences of men have been overgeneralised to include all humanity. In this instance, it seems that the reverse may be the case, i.e. the experiences of birth fathers are less visible and those of birth mothers have been extended or assumed to represent all birth parents. This has led to a conflation of the terms 'birth parent' and 'birth mother'. Two large-scale surveys that refer to 'parents' or 'birth parents' in effect report on the experiences of women. This is because of the small number of birth fathers involved: 13 of 334 in Deykin *et al.* (1984) and 5 of 101 in Hughes and Logan (1993). Although the failure to achieve a statistically relevant response from men is not explicitly given as a reason, Deykin subsequently went on to study birth fathers (Deykin *et al.* 1988). In their work, except for one man, Hughes and Logan draw upon quotes solely from women and switch between use of the two phrases – 'birth parents' and 'birth mothers' (1993, pp.24–25); other writers do the same. Brodzinsky subtitles her literature review 'The Birth Mother Experience', yet the conclusion speaks for both birth fathers and birth mothers:

> The newly found voice of the silent member of the adoption triangle will not rest until some re-evaluation of adoption policy is undertaken. Having offered false hopes and promises in the past, we must now take up the challenge of providing more realistic and more effective modes of intervening with birth parents. (1990, pp.314–315)

Still other researchers alternate the terms in the space of two sentences: 'Birth parents cannot receive anonymity. Giving birth to that child and being that child's mother is a fact of life that cannot be wiped out' (Baran and Pannor 1990, p.329). And:

> The needs of birthparents have been overlooked and need to be redressed. One way would be to provide them with identifying information about their lost children that would offer the 'peace of mind' that so many birthmothers would welcome. (Wells 1993a, p.26)

Further evidence of a conflation of the terms 'birth mother' and 'birth parent' exists in official documents (Scottish Office 1993) and in the writings of adoption practitioners (Post-Adoption Social Workers Group 1987; Sawbridge 1991).

Therefore a specific body of opinion and practice – writings, specialist expertise, knowledge base, advice and information ('dos and don'ts') – is evolving with research and theoretical roots in the experiences of only one of the birth parents involved in the adoption process: the birth mother. For instance in the matter of later-life contact, at present adoption practice is proceeding on the basis of only birth mothers' desire for such meetings (DoH and Welsh Office 1992, p.121). Practice guidelines issued by the UK Government in 2000 ('Intermediary Services for Birth Relatives', DoH 2000c) refers throughout to 'birth parents' whilst only drawing upon research on birth mothers.

The absence of birth fathers in the literature and the existence of somewhat ambivalent attitudes towards them pose the question of how many birth fathers might we be referring to? Whilst we know how many children have been adopted and can assume each one had a birth father and a birth mother, does the invisibility of birth fathers reflect a reality – that generally they fade out of the picture or actively vanish when the going gets tough? Notwithstanding an overall lack of 'visibility' of birth parents (Mullender and Kearn 1997, p.148), the numbers of birth parents that use post-adoption counselling and mental health services show a very small minority of birth fathers (Howe 1990; Hughes and Logan 1993). In the light of this difficulty in establishing a sense of the actual number of birth fathers who might feel they have experienced adoption in a way similar to that of birth mothers, information was obtained from three sources: the two Adoption Contact Registers of England, and Wales and Scottish Contact Register.

Birth Fathers in the Statistics: The UK Adoption Contact Registers

The first Adoption Contact Register (ACR) was established by the charity NORCAP in 1982. Since then ACRs have been established in Scotland (1984) and by The Office of National Statistics (1991). The ACRs function as a means to put adopted people and their birth relatives in touch with each other. Individuals place their names and contact details on these registers and in the event of someone connected with them either already having registered or registering sometime in the future, then contact with each other is arranged. Mullender and Kearn have explored various aspects of the ACRs and one of their findings is that they are under-publicised (1997, p.124). Consequently the overall numbers of people on the various registers are low relative to the theoretical number of those who might use the service. Notwithstanding this reservation, the numbers registered give some indication of the relative proportions of birth mothers and birth fathers on each of the ACRs. Also, it is possible to ascertain the overall number of birth fathers who have 'come out', i.e. have made themselves visible.

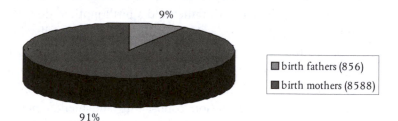

N = 9444

Figure 3.2 NORCAP ACR for England and Wales: Numbers of Birth Parents Registered at January 2001

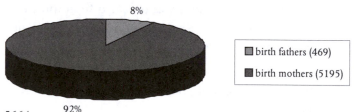

N = 5664

Figure 3.3 Part II of the Office of National Statistics ACR for England and Wales: Numbers of Birth Parents Registered at January 2001

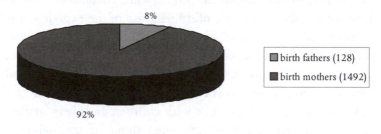

8%

birth fathers (128)
birth mothers (1492)

92%

N = 1620

Figure 3.4 ACR for Scotland: Number of Birth Parents Registered at January 2001

As might be expected, more birth mothers are registered than birth fathers. However, in terms of birth fathers, the proportions are reasonably consistent across all three ACRs showing them as an average of nearly 9 per cent of registered birth parents. Mullender and Kearn's study of Part II of the ACR for England and Wales (1997, p.148) found that birth fathers made up 4.6 per cent of the birth relatives registered, based on figures available as at 1995. It may be that the rise in the percentage of birth fathers registered could be attributed to an increase in publicity surrounding contacts between birth parents and their children (including the meeting of MP Clare Short and her son in October 1996). Other factors could include the rise in general interest in fathers. The fact is that nearly 1500 birth fathers in Scotland, England and Wales have placed their names on ACRs with a view to possible contact with a child that was given up for adoption. This figure alone indicates an interest from more birth fathers than may be supposed.

Thus, it would seem that some birth fathers feel a connection to their child without ever having parented it (and sometimes not having seen the child either). What is the nature of this feeling? Can the experiences of the birth fathers in this study provide more substance to existing birth father accounts of loss and attachment to their children that have been adopted? And where might the experiences of birth fathers fit within a wider framework of men's identity as fathers? A more informed grasp of the experiences of men in adoption may not only contribute to a better understanding of the overall birth parent experience, it may also provide an insight as regards men's perceptions of fatherhood. Despite being a subject of vital importance to policy and law-makers and all who work with children and their families, fatherhood, and especially how men think of themselves as fathers, is something of which we know very little.

Chapter Four

Fatherhood Today

This study looks at the apparent conundrum of men whose only contribution to a child has been a biological one and yet who think of themselves as more than someone who participated in the act of 'fathering', i.e. conception. It will be seen that the experiences and perspectives of many of the men challenge much of contemporary thinking that holds that fatherhood is usually expressed socially, i.e. by men acting in the parental role. Activity is often the sole measure of fatherhood. The question of dimensions of fatherhood other than simply playing the part of father has up-to-date relevance. To cite just one example, there is now the issue of men who are or have been sperm donors and how they may be designated 'father' – if only in the eyes of the child (Blyth 1999; *The Guardian* editorial, 14 October 1999). Government policies and their underlying assumptions often pose a variety of definitions of fatherhood: the biological, legal, social, or biological and social (Lewis 1994; Sarre 1996). In their discussion of the various states of fatherhood Burghes *et al.* ask simply 'Who is the child's father?' (1997). Is it the economic provider as defined by the various elements of child financial support legislation or is it the active parent as defined by the Children's Acts of England and Wales (1989) and Scotland (1995)? Anything other than a cursory examination indicates that at any one time there may be a number of definitions of fatherhood being relied upon by policy makers. Given the inter-relationship of policy and public opinion, a brief look at changing societal perceptions of fathers is necessary.

Fathers – A Recent History

A major shift in societal attitudes to fathers has taken place since the 1950s: it is generally agreed that a more involved form of parenting is expected of men (Cabrera *et al*. 2000; Burgess 1997; Burghes *et al*. 1997). Pasley and Minton note that 'men today are being asked to become more involved in the care of their children' (1997, p.121). Recent studies of fathers have found a congruence between this greater societal endorsement of a more involved type of fathering and the child care practices of fathers (Dienhart 1998; Lupton and Barclay 1997). Doherty observes that 'there probably has never been a time when more fathers were involved in the daily nurturing of their children' (1997, p.220). However the experiences of the men in this study began in a different period; 1952 was the time of earliest birth father experience.

Fifty years ago societal expectations of fathers – during pregnancy and childbirth, of their involvement in childcare and domestic tasks – were less. Fathers were generally excluded from the birth of their children (Davidoff *et al*. 1999, p.209). Men were expected to play the role of breadwinner, whilst women's part was to be that of the homemaker (*ibid*. p.197). Fathers were designated 'mothers' supporters' (Blendis 1982) and:

> ...the dominant, though not exclusive, cultural image of the twentieth century father has been the 'father-breadwinner model' wherein fathers were the ultimate sources of both morality and discipline but physically, socially and emotionally removed from the family by their concentration on work. (Cohen 1993, p.2)

These ideas continued throughout the 1960s and 70s. Twenty years ago Lewis wrote of 'the dislocation of males from the world of child rearing [that] occurs as a natural course of events' (1982, p.51). Lewis also found that in 1970, 40 per cent of UK fathers of very young children came home to a sleeping child during the week 'whilst today [the eighties] only 25 per cent of employed fathers are not home before 7pm and babies may be staying up later – especially when mothers work, too' (*ibid.*). Irrespective of whether reality has changed in terms of men's involvement in child care (Edwards 1998), *ideas* that endorse fathers' greater involvement in pregnancy and child care have increased substantially over the last 50 years.

Fathers Now

The end of the 20th and beginning of the 21st century has seen a period of renewed interest in fatherhood. The literature is burgeoning (Marsiglio *et al.* 2000), 'fathers and fatherhood are in vogue' (Burghes *et al.* 1997) and popular culture has a 'fascination' with fatherhood (Dienhart 1998). The media have gone through a period of referring to fathers as either 'new men' or 'feckless' –'dead-beat dads' is the US version of feckless fathers (Bradshaw *et al.* 1999; Burgess and Ruxton 1996; Sarre 1996). Often fathers have been characterised as either 'heroes or villains' (Burgess 1997; Mason 1995). Young unmarried fathers have been singled out especially (Speak, Cameron and Gilroy 1997). *The Guardian* described the tone of these discussions as something of a 'moral panic' (16 June 1999). Predictably more heat than light has been generated by media discussions yet they form a social backdrop and inform popular attitudes to fathers and fatherhood.

Comments and speeches of UK Government figures have sometimes contributed to these negative elements (Bradshaw *et al.* 1999; Sarre 1996). However, governments in the UK and the USA have also moved to support fathers, particularly those who are young and unmarried (Department of Health 1999; Griswold 1998). The establishment of the National Family and Parenting Institute (Department of Health 1999) indicates that the subjects of parenting, fathers and fatherhood are high on the UK Government agenda (Burgess and Ruxton 1996; Family Policy Unit 1998; Speak *et al.* 1997). Government and public attention has often concentrated upon certain *types* of father: these include unmarried fathers, teenage fathers, non-resident fathers and biological fathers (Lewis 2000). Each type has its own individual discourse, however negative discourses may overlap as in the case of young unmarried fathers – 'the feckless boys' in the words of Melanie Phillips (*The Observer*, 26 April 1998), living apart from the mother and child (Speak *et al.* 1997). The findings of Speak *et al.* (1997) regarding the circumstances of young unmarried fathers in Newcastle and similar work of others (Edinburgh Family Service Unit 2001; Rolphe 1999; The Princes Trust, 2001) have provided a better informed and more positive picture. This includes evidence of young unmarried fathers' feelings of commitment to their children and the material obstacles that serve to prevent expressions of this, e.g. money for bus fares.

'Absent fathers' are another group of fathers who have come in for substantial discussion; 'non-resident fathers' is probably a less pejorative and more accurate term (Simpson, McCarthy and Walker 1995). Here a number of negative generalisations feature. In the case of non-resident fathers, an oft-quoted statistic is that of the '40% rule' (Bradshaw *et al.* 1999; Burgess 1997; Hill 1998; Milligan and Dowie 1998). This is a conclusion drawn from research into the proportion of fathers said to lose contact with their children after separation (Bradshaw and Millar 1991). This research and similar findings in the USA (Furstenberg and Cherlin 1991; Furstenberg *et al.* 1983) point to the prevalence of diminishing contact between children and their fathers when the latter separate from their partners.

However, as in the case of young unmarried fathers, subsequent research has questioned such negative generalisations. Burgess has described conclusions drawn from the '40% rule' as the 'myth of the disappearing dad' and has questioned the methodology of the UK research (1997, p.192). For instance she points out that the research asked the lone parent (with custody) about the absent one, thus omitting the absent parent's version of contact arrangements. Work by Bradshaw and others (Bradshaw *et al.* 1999) on the basis of a study of over six hundred non-resident fathers, has re-evaluated the original Bradshaw and Millar (1991) research findings. These new findings provide evidence of 'a much higher level of contact than that derived from studies of lone parents (i.e. the parent resident with the child)' (1999, p.81). The reasons for the apparent discrepancy between the findings in 1991 and those of the 1999 study include the earlier study's emphasis on contact as *seeing* the child. The authors of the 1999 study point out that this 'may be, with hindsight, too imprecise a definition of contact' (p.82), i.e. the first study omitted to include contact by phone and letter.

When the various discourses on fathers and fatherhood are examined the paucity of our knowledge of fatherhood becomes clear and various confusions and contradictions come to light (Burghes *et al.* 1997). These are chiefly concerning the respective positions of: the social and biological father, the social father only, and the biological father only. Fatherhood is decidedly a central concern to policy makers (Burghes *et al.* 1997) however Government policies have not been coherent. For instance, the Children's Act (England and Wales) 1989 appeared to automatically confer paternal obligations upon the social father (unless a biological father applied for parental responsibility) and yet two years later the Child Support Act (CSA 1991) seemed to suggest something different. The CSA appears to regard the biological father as the father who is responsible (financially speaking) for the child (Burghes *et al.* 1997; Sarre 1996).

Sarre notes a similar lack of coherence in the UK 1979 Law Commission Report on Illegitimacy. In the same document, 'Biological links were supported by the promotion of automatic parental responsibility, and social links were supported by the recommendations on AID [artificial insemination by donor]' (*ibid.* p.43). A theme 'that arises time and time again is whether fatherhood should be defined biologically or socially' and in this matter 'policy makers have varied on which fathers have been dealt with' (*ibid.* p.44). Policy makers may be reflecting a wider set of contradictions because in law 'there is no one fatherhood' (Collier 1995, p.184). Lewis notes that 'it is possible to be any one, or any combination of these types of father [biological, social or legal] in different legal systems' (1994, p.2). Additionally, new complexities and diversities such as advances in reproductive technology have 'forced an appraisal of what constitutes fatherhood in our society' (Sarre 1996, p.41).

As we shall see, the literature on fatherhood has mushroomed and as the research community has sought to address the question of fatherhood, questions about the function of fathers are now a regular feature (Daniels 1998; Eggebeen and Knoester 2001; Lamb 1996; Williams 1998). Typically Burghes *et al.* (1997) ask 'What do we really know of fathers and fatherhood?' Despite this growth in interest it will be seen that there is little consensus in the literature as to the nature of fatherhood (Burghes *et al.* 1997; Pasley and Minton 1997; Tanfer and Mott 1998). This lack of research consensus mirrors the wider public, legal and policy lack of clarity. Furthermore, the research that has taken place has a number of limitations. Fatherhood research has generally not explored men's definitions of what they believe constitutes fatherhood. Second, the research has been mainly confined to men who either are, or intend to be, both biological and social fathers, and finally the majority of the research on fathers tends to focus upon what fathers do with their children, i.e. fathering as an activity.

The preponderance of heat over light in public discussions of what constitutes the various types of fatherhood and the respective obligations that come with these, a lack of coherence in policy attitudes towards social and biological fatherhood, and what Bradshaw *et al.* refer to as a 'remarkable reassertion of the obligations of biological fathers' (1999, p.228), point to a need to explore biological fatherhood. The issue would seem to be worthy of considerable research interest yet the present state of our knowledge is not as extensive as we may imagine.

Fatherhood – Some Unanswered Questions

At a societal level there is 'public intrigue with the positive and negative aspects of fatherhood' (Marsiglio 1995a). Matters such as what constitutes fatherhood are under the 'public gaze' (Lewis 1995) including such issues as men's financial and emotional involvement with their children. There are popular stereotypes of men as cruel or absent fathers; debate continues as to the various meanings of the term 'absent fathers' (Bradshaw *et al.* 1999) and the extent to which the description of fecklessness is accurate as applied to young unmarried fathers (Burgess 1997; Freeley 1999). Despite a widespread interest, the subject of fatherhood remains one about which there are more ideas and opinions than empirical research.

Although there has been a growth over the past 25 years (Tanfer and Mott 1998), the overall knowledge base on fatherhood and fathers remains small (Edwards 1998; Shapiro *et al.* 1995). Research findings are lacking in consensus about the nature and meaning of fatherhood (Clarke and Popay 1998; Lewis 2000; Marsiglio 1995a). Lewis comments that debates have been dominated by an 'economic view' of fathering, i.e. man as breadwinner (Lewis 2000). Clarke and Popay note that 'the actual meanings and definitions attached by men to fatherhood and their personal experiences of fathering are unclear from the literature' (1998, p.203). They go on to remark that: 'Although there has been a ground-swell of research and empirical studies, we still have little knowledge of how most men perceive fatherhood' (*ibid.*). The private lives of fathers remain 'largely hidden' (Burgess and Ruxton 1996, v).

Much of the existing research has explored what fathers do – or do not do (Lewis 1986). Relatively little exists about what being a father *is* and how men perceive of themselves in this capacity – where fatherhood fits in a man's identity and men's perceptions of themselves as fathers. Fathering in its widest sense is little researched (Lewis 2000). For instance, research has rarely explored matters of how men become fathers (Burgess 1997; La Rossa 1986; Lewis 1982; May 1982) or sought to examine fatherhood as a concept (McKee and O'Brien 1982a). Roopnarine and Miller argue that the exact beginning of fatherhood is ambiguous and that: 'Few studies have explicitly examined fathers' transition to parenthood, and none has focused on the impact of pregnancy' (1985, p.50).

The question of what fatherhood is then, and the meanings that are lent to it by men, have been neglected in favour of the more technical question of what fathers do. Men have rarely been asked what they think fatherhood consists of. Neither, in the main, have researchers explored the various dimensions of fatherhood other than its practical expression in 'hands-on' parenting. So what can the existing research on fathers contribute to this study of a particular group of fathers – men who have had no social contact with the child in question?

Key Themes in Fatherhood Research and Literature

As noted, the literature and research focusing on fatherhood has grown considerably since 1975 when Lamb remarked that fathers were 'the forgotten contributors to child development' (1987, xiii). Until the 1970s there was a scarcity of social science research on fatherhood (Barber 1975; McKee and O'Brien 1982b; Richards 1982). From the 1980s onward research and writing on fatherhood has gathered speed and there is now a 'voluminous body of work' (Marsiglio *et al.* 2000). Two key themes emerge as relevant to any study of birth fathers.

The Beginnings of Fatherhood

The popular convention is that 'most men embark on parenthood nine months later than their womenfolk' ('Baby Blues…For Dad' *The Guardian*, 27 September 1995). This notion is reflected in the academic discussion in which substantive fatherhood is held to begin at birth once the man becomes able to physically care for the baby (Daniels and Weingarten 1982; Greenberg 1985; Lewis 1986; Seel 1987). Interestingly, some of the adoption literature also suggests this gulf or vacuum between conception and the appearance of a child (Tugendhat 1992; Departmental Committee on the Adoption of Children 1970; Sawbridge 1980). Rowe's belief that 'differentiation of parenting from the act of giving birth is probably an essential part of genuine acceptance of adoption' (1977, p.92) implies that being a parent is what is done after birth. In the minority are other writers (Diamond 1995a; La Rossa 1986) who have argued that the process of becoming a father begins *before* conception.

Thus, the majority view is that fatherhood begins when there's something to do: 'becoming a father has meant becoming a social father more than a biological father' (Burgess 1997, p.120). In short fathers come into their own only when their child is born thus enabling them to act as fathers. However, an effect of this concentration on what men do in social interaction with a child 'obscures other aspects of fatherhood' such as thoughts and emotions (Dienhart 1998, p.28). Specific literature on expectant fatherhood and in particular, discussion of any pre-birth consciousness of fatherhood is scarce (Federal Interagency Forum on Child and Family Statistics 1998; Gurwitt 1995; May 1995). What exists is either selective, focusing as it does upon pathological reactions to pregnancy or marital relations, or is concerned with men's transition to adulthood. The selectivity of some studies has been noted – concentrating as they have on men's abnormal or pathological reactions to pregnancy (Beail 1982; Lewis 1986; Richman 1982). Other studies have been confined to the man's role as husband and partner and not specifically as a father (Lewis 1986; Richards 1982).

Little material appears to address the question of fatherhood in relation to the unborn child. Here the research seems mostly concerned with the male's emotional and psychological transition to adulthood and maturity. From the perspective of psychological growth, much is made of pregnancy (for men) as containing potential for individual development. For instance May argues that 'the processes of psychological and social adaptation during pregnancy are probably as significant in men as they are in women' (1995, p.93). Other studies describe expectant first-time fathers as having grown up, becoming more responsible, mature and having an opportunity for emotional involvement (Lewis 1986; Owens 1982; Seel 1987). When the literature has addressed expectant fathers' inner worlds, it has tended to concentrate on personal and psychological growth as distinct from any attention to possible developments in the father's relationship with the unborn child. Indeed Lewis has challenged any notion of a specific male 'pregnancy'. He observes that 'men necessarily experience pregnancy and birth through their wives' (1982, p.67). This view contrasts with that of others who suggest a 'biological essence' to the expectant fatherhood experience (Krampe and Fairweather 1993) and Mead, who notes that 'expectant fathers often have certain biochemical responses during their wives' pregnancies' (1962, p.53). Others acknowledge gender difference, e.g. the lack of biological immediacy (Diamond 1995a, p.269). However it is also argued that the father's 'protective agency', e.g. the provision of a 'timely and nurturing holding environment' (Diamond 1995b, p.245) is an equally meaningful counterpart to the mother's 'maternal biological contact, feeding and attunement' (Diamond *ibid.* p.246).

There have been other suggestions of a unique relationship between father-to-be and unborn child. Expectant fathers may forge special 'bonds' with the unborn child via 'nesting' activities, and shopping for baby goods (Richman 1982, p.100). Other writers have identified a deeper emotionally empathic responsiveness – the development of a 'watchful protectiveness' (Diamond 1995b, p.25). This emerges in pregnancy and helps to provide a good beginning for the father's infant child. This is seen as part of an expectant father's 'protective agency' (*ibid.* p.246) and taken together with the provision of material necessities, reflects what is described as the 'psychobiological instinctual basis of fathering' (Benedek 1970 quoted in Diamond 1995a, p.269).

Diamond, (1995a, 1995b) draws on the work of Wolson (1995) to outline a concept of the expectant 'holding father' in possession of an 'adaptive grandiosity', which entails the father's projection of his 'special, ideal self' onto his child as well as a capacity to differentiate himself from his baby. This 'ideal' father then develops and maintains an empathic sensitivity with his baby and his wife as separate individuals. Diamond cites Benedek's theory of an instinctive 'psychobiology' of fatherhood:

> Fatherhood (i.e. the male's role in procreation) has instinctual roots beyond the drive organisation of mating behaviour. She (Benedek) believed these roots included both his function as a provider and a capacity to develop *fatherliness ties* that render his relationship to his children a mutual developmental experience. (1995a, p.270; emphasis in original)

Such a capacity for 'fatherliness ties' would suggest that 'a father's actual *attachment and relationship* to his infant commences long before labour and delivery' (Diamond 1995a, p.279; emphasis in original). In short, in relation to expectant parenthood for men, an absence of the processes and experiences that are undergone by women (conception, pregnancy, birth) may not automatically preclude men from feeling connected with their unborn children.

Thus this work of Diamond (1995a and 1995b), also Hawkins *et al.* (1995), Marsiglio (1995b) Motluk (2000) and Mackey (2001) on the instinctual basis of fathering and the ability of expectant fathers to form a relationship with the unborn child is an advance in contemporary theorising in relation to expectant fathers. It is also helpful in efforts to chart the emergence of a consciousness of fatherhood in men – whether or not their 'path' continues to active parenting. Overall however there is a scarcity of insight as to the consciousness of expectant fathers *vis-à-vis* any relationship with their unborn child (May 1995; Mercer *et al.* 1988). Certainly there seems to be nothing about how birth fathers might experience a connection to their adopted children.

The second area of fatherhood studies that is relevant to birth fathers is the existence of deep-seated assumptions regarding fathers and mothers and the place of the child (unborn or otherwise) in their thoughts.

Fathering and Mothering

Conventionally speaking, a man 'fathers' a child only by participation in the act of conception. Typically, fathering a child is put thus: 'Fathering my son took a couple of glasses of wine and a raise of the eyebrow' (Matthew Engels in *The Guardian Weekend*, 29 May 1999). See also Brodzinsky's reference to 'individuals who father a child' (1990, p.315). The standard dictionary definition of 'to father' is to beget or sire a child (Johnson 1988). The term fathering is not normally employed to convey caring, being committed or any emotional bond with a child unborn or otherwise (Lewis 2000). Thus a man is not engaged in 'fathering' his children when he takes them to school or nurses their various ailments. In doing these things he may be described as 'parenting' but even this term is clumsy when applied to men's actions with their children (Ross 1982). In order to show how conventional thinking regards men, researchers have pointed to the difference between women who look after their children and men who 'baby-sit' when their partner goes out (Hawkins *et al.* 1995). Whilst maternity and motherhood are established, the concept of paternity is 'more tenuous' (Sarre 1996, p.1). Sarre also points to a 'conflation' between parenting, nurturing and mothering which constructs men *and* women in a biological essentialist framework, i.e. women automatically have a proclivity and ability to care, with the converse being the case for men (see also La Rossa 1986). Richards argues that:

Many questions about the ways in which the distinct male and female reproductive physiology may (or may not) give rise to differing expectations and experiences of parenthood for men and women remain to be explored. (1982, p.57)

Much of the research and writing on fathering and fatherhood has questioned the powerful social convention and stereotype that 'while notions of paternity often embody an idea of the acquisition of property, maternity is more related to concepts of giving and fulfilment' (*ibid.*). The idea that parenthood is equated with motherhood only (Dienhart 1998; Williams and Robertson 1999) has been the concern of many writers since at least the early 1970s when Rutter commented that 'a less exclusive focus on the mother is required. Children also have fathers!' (1972, p.125). Recent UK research on young unmarried non-resident fathers also confirms men's ability to feel a paternal commitment in spite of the constraints of physical distance and lack of day-to-day familiarity (Speak *et al.* 1997). However this field of research on fatherhood and fathers' activities (the latter being in the overall majority) has a number of shortcomings. It has been pointed out that fathers' private lives remain largely hidden and that there are only limited accounts of fatherhood from fathers themselves (Burgess 1997; Clarke and Popay 1998; Dienhart 1998). A few writers have also observed that the singular world of men's consciousness of themselves as fathers has been neglected and that the agenda for fatherhood has not been set independently of motherhood (Burghes *et al.* 1997; Richards 1982). It has been suggested that in writings on fathers, there is a pro-natalist or biologically essentialist tendency that tends to view fathers as male mothers (Dienhart 1998; Lupton and Barclay 1997), or motherhood as something that men can aspire too but cannot achieve. For instance: 'It is unusual for children to be closer to fathers than mothers because they are made inside their mothers. We men are not equal, we are a secondary parent'

(Sebastian Kraemer, child and family psychiatrist, *The Observer*, 21 April 1996).

It seems therefore that the general research on fatherhood is limited in the insights it may offer. First, there is a scarcity of knowledge regarding the totality of men's experience from their awareness of pregnancy and conception, to birth and beyond. Second, there is little that explores the inner world of fathers, especially fathers-to-be. Because of these research gaps our thinking on fatherhood is limited and conventional opinion remains locked in stereotypes of both what women are born to and what men are not, in terms of parenthood. At worst, fathering is the one-off act of siring a child (Burgess 1997). It is perhaps not surprising then that men, who have had or will have no contact with their child, might be marginalised from the decision-making processes in matters such as adoption.

In noting an early differentiation between fathers and mothers based upon the assumption that fathering follows the birth, Brinich suggests that this may be a 'stereotypical view of the development of fatherhood'. Brinich goes on to call for a re-examination of this view and concludes that research with men who have fathered children who were then relinquished for adoption 'would yield much more than the vacuum that previous authors have suggested exists' (1990, p.59). The discussion of fatherhood has shown that our knowledge is limited. Our knowledge of birth fathers is even less. On both counts the narratives of the birth fathers in this study can contribute to our existing understandings. In addition, the study goes toward filling the vacuum that exists in respect of how fatherhood may develop – and continue.

Part II

The Life Experiences
of Birth Fathers

'… it's a bit of me that I have allowed nobody else to get close to. I mean this two and quarter hours is the most in all those 30 odd years that I've ever had. I've never talked about some of the things in terms of the feelings that I've shared here today.'

Chapter Five

The Birth Fathers, the Pregnancy and the Birth of the Child

Thirty Birth Fathers – the Study

There were two qualifications for inclusion in the study. First, that the birth fathers were involved in a *baby* adoption, i.e. children up to the age of one year as distinct from the adoption of children of an older age. Second, that the adoptions had taken place outside the family circle or close relatives, i.e. the adoptive parents were strangers and consequently the man would have no knowledge of the child's upbringing or welfare. Although the numbers of baby adoptions have been falling and the numbers of children adopted at an older age rising, it is those in the former group (baby adoptions) that have been the focus for the vast majority of interest and work to date. This has come about as a result of various factors. These include the changing climate in favour of less secrecy in the adoption process and changes in legislation relating to birth records (The Children Acts of 1975 and 1989, England and Wales) that have led to adopted children, now adult, seeking and making contact with their birth parents. Researching birth fathers in an analogous position to the birth mothers in existing birth mother studies ensures that the two sets of experiences can be compared. Furthermore, the theoretical question of whether or not there is any sense of fatherhood relinquished – and whether something of this remains for the birth father – would be skewed and the research over-expanded by 'allowing in' those fathers who had participated in raising a child that had subsequently been adopted.

There is no straightforward means of contacting birth fathers who have had a child adopted. There is no requirement that unmarried fathers (the vast majority of such birth fathers) be registered on a child's birth certificate. Also some men may not know that they are birth fathers, i.e. they may be unaware of the pregnancy, birth, adoption or all three (as was at least one man in this study). Consequently such men may not appear in agency files and records. The problems in identifying birth fathers who may be willing to be interviewed can be seen in figures relating to birth parent use of post-adoption services. One agency cites 96 per cent of their birth parent service users as being women (Howe 1990). Previous birth father responses to explicit calls for help have also been negligible (Powell and Warren 1997; Tugendhat 1992).

The birth fathers in this study were found from a limited population that had been in touch with post-adoption agencies or saw an advertisement in an associated magazine. In this respect they were 'visible' – they had already indicated that they were open to contact, they were actively seeking this or had an interest in reading about other birth parents. In this sense the men, although most did not term themselves birth fathers, identified themselves as having some connection with and interest in their adopted child. However, men who do not express such feelings and take no steps to make contact with their child may not be uncommitted; it will be seen that four of the study group were unexpectedly traced. But it is important to note that the majority of the views of the men in this study are drawn from a group of fathers who had already shown some form of interest – if only by registering on an Adoption Contact Register (ACR) – in their child. It should also be noted that the existing research on birth mothers is also characterised by this bias with participants being identified because of their contact with post-adoption services (Edwards and Williams 2000; Kalmuss, Namerow and Cushman 1991).

Once the men had responded to a letter asking for their assistance an interview was arranged in their homes. The men lived throughout the UK – from the north of Scotland to the south east of England, in housing estates and the Home Counties stockbroker belt – unemployed drivers, businessmen and white-collar professionals were interviewed. One man was a musician, another a church minister; another man was a Justice of the Peace. Another spoke to me in his retirement home. All the men were either white Scottish or English and were aged between 35 and 79 (median: 50). At the time of the interview, 23 were married or in relationships. Four of the latter group of men were married to or living with the birth mother at the time of the interview – two sets of birth mothers and birth fathers had been together since the adoption. Two had recently come together again. Three of the 23 men in relationships were going through separations. The remaining seven men were single (previously widowed, divorced or separated); three of this group had had multiple divorces. At the time of the birth a majority of the men were in their late teens.

Twenty-six of the men knew of the birth at the time with the other four finding out some weeks and months afterwards. Fifteen of the men saw and held their child; for most this took place once and briefly at the hospital. There was no further contact with the child. Four men had had previous children. In all 21 went on to parent after the adoption. Nine men had no children subsequent to the adoption; for five of these men the adopted child was their only one.

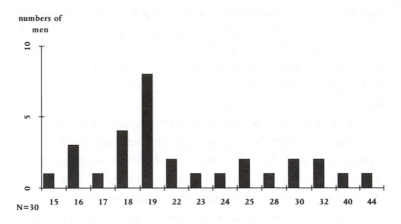

Figure 5.1 Ages of the Men at Time of Birth of Child

The Interviews

In a study that invites the narrator to present a retrospective life review, the narrator's weighting, impressions and manner of presentation of an issue may shift over time (Yow 1994, p.172). Such shifts are inevitable as processes such as maturation and the effect of other life experiences, e.g. loss and parenthood, change attitudes to questions such as obligation and responsibility (Cicchini 1993). In some respects it is self-evident that the men's experiences – such as subsequently becoming fathers and parenting a child – would have an influence on their accounts and produce the possibility of varying interpretations of the same events depending upon when the interview took place. As it is self-evident that subsequent parenting experiences can colour and shift elements in narratives, so too is it obvious that the narrators exist in a social and cultural context in which attitudes to fathers and paternal involvement have changed over the 30 years since many of the adoptions. For example if the men had been interviewed at the beginning of the 1970s instead of the late 1990s, the cultural and societal norms then may have produced less emphasis on their notions of fatherhood than exists within their narratives today:

> Because of shifts in fatherhood, fathers may have been reluctant in the past to admit to too much involvement in child care and domestic activities; now they may be reluctant to admit too little. (Burghes *et al.* 1997, p.55)

If this is the case with the men in the study, then the data is not invalidated or untruthful. Rather what is available is the men's truths now, looking back over lives that incorporate both subsequent influential experiences and societal changes. The rest of this chapter and the remainder of the chapters on the life experiences of the birth fathers present a chronological account of those experiences. A chapter has been given over to each phase, e.g. 'The Pregnancy and The Birth'. In the course of the chapters comparisons will be made with other research such as that on birth mothers. Each chapter concludes with a summary and discussion of the themes and issues that have emerged.

The Pregnancy

> salient: arresting, conspicuous, important, jutting, marked, noticeable, outstanding, projecting, prominent, pronounced, protruding, remarkable, signal, striking. (Collins Thesaurus 1991)

A combination of powerful events and experiences produced deep and lasting feelings for almost all of the 30 men in the group. The adoption 'looms large' in their lives many years later. In the words of another: 'The adoption has formed my reaction to a number of things in my life'. The adoption, seen as a process of events, experiences and feelings during pregnancy, surrounding the birth of their child, the adoption itself and in the weeks and months following the adoption, has an emotional salience. Events for most began with news of the pregnancy.

'Going Steady'

The time between news of the pregnancy and the birth of the child was emotionally turbulent. Powerful mixtures of pleasure and pain, commitment and loss, inclusion and exclusion are present during this period. The first threads of a feeling of fatherhood are also in evidence for some.

Twenty-five men said that they and the birth mother had been in a stable relationship. This is defined as committed to one another and 'going steady' for more than three months. Two of these men were married to the birth mother. Two others described the relationship as brief or new. Two more men were involved with or married to someone else. One man said his relationship with the birth mother was 'superficial' – although he and she were living together. The finding that so many of these birth fathers and birth mothers had been in a stable relationship with each other goes very much against the stereotype of young mothers whose babies are adopted after a brief association with the father. Hughes and Logan (1993) and Wells (1993b) refer to the birth mother's relationship with the birth father in their research and also challenge the conventional notion of adoptions following pregnancies after 'one night stands' between relative strangers. However most of the literature on birth mothers does not enquire into or assess the relationship between birth mother and birth father. One of the most widely-regarded works expressly sought out women who were partnerless at the time of the adoption (Winkler and van Keppel 1984).

There are a small number of reports that discuss birth fathers' attitudes to the pregnancy (Bouchier *et al.* 1991; Inglis 1984; Mander 1995; Raynor 1971). The following comment is not atypical in its tendency to dismiss the birth father:

> In other cases he was a married man or a feckless, insubstantial individual that the woman did not wish to marry... With the increasing urgency of sorting out what to do and where to go, the birth father became of less interest and relevance. As the birth mother necessarily became preoccupied with her own

worries, he would find that there was little room in the saga for him and often he completely disappeared from the story. This upset and angered some mothers but not a few viewed his departure neutrally and with no great interest. (Howe *et al.* 1992, p.54)

Most of the observations in such writings agree with Mander's conclusion that once the pregnancy was confirmed, the birth father was of 'relatively minor significance'. The accounts that follow will show that, for a large majority of the study group, negative or unsupported assumptions such as these do not hold true.

Pregnancy: The Emotional Response

Because of the steady nature of their relationship with the birth mother, most of the men were aware of the pregnancy within two months of conception. The news of pregnancy was met with a variety of reactions and emotions. The most common was one of shock. Over half of the group (15) described shock or alarm on news of the pregnancy; six used the word 'shock'. Another three said that the news had made them feel scared and anxious. A further three felt a mixture of shock and fear with other feelings of anxiety. Three more initially felt worry. These feelings were experienced primarily because of the unplanned nature of the event together with fear of the repercussions. In three cases either the birth mother, birth father or both were under-age. One man was, 'Shocked like any young man of 19. You think "Oh my God what have I done?" or "What have we done?" I was frightened of the consequences. Frightened of parents'. For others looking back, the worry was because of their lack of maturity:

> I think she kept hoping that her period would start and she was four months before we went to the doctor. I always remember that night and he said 'Yes, yes' and took her into the room and came back out and 'yes, yes, she's definitely pregnant'. I thought 'Christ, that's what I don't want to hear'. He said 'She's

fine, no problem, very healthy' and I said 'Well there's a problem' I said 'We're not married'. 'Oh that's no problem', he said. I said 'I'm 16'. The doctor then said 'Ah well that could be a problem'.

Elsewhere there was concern because 'It was taboo, I was immature and with low wages, it was difficult to look after a kid'. Six men were pleased. Two in this group were married to the birth mother and therefore there was an element of planning involved with regard to conception and parenthood. Another five men underwent a mixture of competing feelings such as unhappiness and pleasure and fear (of parents) and pride. One felt 'Unhappy – I thought "How's her family going to react?" Also pleasure – I'm going to be a dad – and sadness at the (birth) mother's family hostility'. Another man experienced:

> A tremendous mixture of feelings really. Sadness because it wasn't planned. I remember it was in my final year. There was obviously a conflict of feelings. But very mixed emotions. I suppose initially shocked, sad. Worried about what we were going to do, how we were going to cope with the situation.

Four men responded to the news of the pregnancy with clearer, negative reactions: one 'did a moonlight'. One man was angry at what he perceived to be manipulation (into marriage). Another expressed disbelief in relation to his paternity of the unborn child and the fourth 'didn't think of the child' at that point because he and the birth mother had separated and he was about to get married to someone else. Overall then, few men responded to the news with undiluted pleasure.

The particular question of birth mothers' reaction to their pregnancy appears to have been discussed infrequently in the research. Where it has been discussed, birth mothers' reactions evidence the same range of panic and alarm as those of the men in the group. This is together with (not explicitly reported by the men in the study group) feelings of shame and guilt at 'having got themselves into trouble' (Inglis 1984).

Pregnancy: A Sense of Fatherhood

At the time of receiving the news and for the remainder of the pregnancy 12 men experienced stirrings of fatherhood. One man was 'looking forward to being able to take him out and do things'. Another said something similar: 'Looking forward to doing things with him. You feel very proud that you are a father. We had made plans'. Although shocked at the news of the pregnancy, one said that:

> We agreed to keep the baby. There was no question of running away. We both agreed that we desperately wanted to keep the baby. Yes, I saw myself as a father. I always thought I was good with kids.

A number with these affirmative feelings towards fatherhood expressed these in a 'workmanlike' approach to the news of the impending birth and child, i.e. although surprised and shocked, they intended and expected to be the child's parent. One of the men asked of himself 'Is this the point in time when you start to settle down?'

During the course of the pregnancy a further three men (who initially answered in the negative when asked whether they had felt like a father) began to experience a sense of curiosity, responsibility or obligation *vis-à-vis* the unborn child. In the case of one, his shock and worry at the news of the birth mother's pregnancy changed to curiosity: 'Both of us began to wonder what the child might be like – we came from families of academics and swimmers – would he or she be sporty, academic?' For these men, paternal feelings emerged and grew as the pregnancy developed:

> Eventually you start feeling you're going to be a dad and it was going to come into the world and you were going to do right by it, there's a maturity comes over you.

One man began 'looking forward to settling down. There had always been kids around. Having children was a natural thing'.

During this time, for almost all, irrespective of their feelings and attitude towards paternity (whether these were present from the start, developed, or remained 'unfatherly') there was a wide range of emotions:

> You think first running away, then you think of your responsibilities, you want to keep a family, you think of yourself at nineteen, you say to yourself 'I've got a whole life'. To me you're swung between running away and staying and facing the music.

The 15 men who spoke of feeling like fathers were asked to elaborate upon this. Two men spoke in terms of ownership – they felt that the child-to-be was theirs – one referred to her as 'My birthday present', for another: 'The baby was mine and my responsibility'. Four spoke of pride in their child's conception and its development during pregnancy: 'I could feel it kicking'. Four spoke of an anticipation of parenting: 'looking forward to doing things'. Five expressed a joint responsibility for the child's conception and talked of their involvement throughout the pregnancy and a wish to become a parent of the child: 'I think we wanted to get married. We'd have managed somehow. I've a great love for children, somehow or other I'd have managed'.

Those birth fathers who said that they had had no feelings of fatherhood (nine) felt they had been too young to think of themselves as fathers: 'I think I was still a big boy at that time. Too young to contemplate, to accept the full consequences of what was going to be'. Or they were committed to other plans that excluded having a child:

> Neither she nor I wanted to have the baby. We were very much in love with each other as these things go. A very good relationship. But we certainly didn't want to have children. I was going to go to College. It came around the time I should have been revising A levels.

For the others who felt no sense of fatherhood, the relationship with the birth mother had ended or according to them it could not sustain the responsibilities of marriage and raising a child.

One man fits the stereotype of the male's immediate abandonment of a pregnant girl friend. In his case, news of the pregnancy resulted in him 'Doing a moonlight. To avoid responsibility. I was immature'. Apart for him, stereotypes of the man's immediate desertion on news of pregnancy, the 'one night stand' or older male sophisticate who gets a young girl in trouble (Pannor *et al.* 1971) do not hold true. Even the 'moonlighter', whilst in the midst of his abandonment of the birth mother, wanted the birth mother to leave her parents' house so that he could return and live independently with her. He also offered to 'keep' (in the financial sense) the child.

Over a half (15/24) of the men who reported on whether or not they felt like fathers during this period replied in the affirmative either from the onset or as the pregnancy developed. Of the remaining six men in the entire group, three birth fathers were not precisely aware of the pregnancy, two could not say how they felt and one omitted to answer. For the most part there seems to be no direct association between those men who were shocked or displeased at news of the pregnancy nor felt like fathers, and whether they did or did not remain involved. However, as we shall see, participation – irrespective of whether he felt like a father or not – was to become problematic for many.

Birth mothers do not seem to have been asked whether or not they felt like mothers during the pregnancy. Howe *et al.* (1992, p.38) move from 'the moment she discovers that she is pregnant' to commence the remainder of their discussion of pregnancy with 'The Unmarried Mother-To-Be'. The assumption being that pregnancy automatically and unproblematically confers motherhood. Wider research has shown that equating pregnancy and motherhood is an overgeneralisation that fails to appreciate the problems surrounding the transition from pregnant woman to mother-to-be (Chodorow 1978; Forna 1998). The research gap in the birth mother literature precludes comparison between birth mother and birth father feelings towards respectively, maternity and paternity.

During the Course of the Pregnancy

Whilst a number of men talked of the growth of feelings of fatherhood during the course of the pregnancy, events of a more external nature also took place. It was difficult to pin down details of this nine-month period in the men's lives. In the quest for information concerning their feelings and behaviour what is gleaned can be at the expense of people and events that surround the birth father. A certain amount of background 'colour' is lost, e.g. many significant world events took place in the 1960s: men landed on the moon (1969) and in Paris in 1968 students nearly brought down the French government. Two men offered such a backdrop when they spoke of being involved in battles between 'mods' and 'rockers' and college sit-ins. Taking my own experience as a reference point, in the course of the pregnancy there were many events – some exciting, some boring – that had little to do with the impending birth. I, and I surmise many of the birth fathers in the study, did 'young people' things such as looking for employment, going to the pub and cinema, being bored as well as attending sessions at the hospital and buying items for a baby's layette. Notwithstanding their inevitably selective nature, the accounts provide some relevant insights relating to life between the initial news of the pregnancy and the birth.

After confirmation of the pregnancy, the next months were marked for ten men (a third of whole group) by either being separated from the birth mother against their will immediately or at a subsequent point in the pregnancy (for five). Or in the case of the other five men, having had no choice about being apart. Three of this latter group were in the armed forces and two were confined: one in prison and the other in a reform school. An example of the feelings of powerlessness in the events of this period is provided in the case of one of the men who was in the armed forces and serving overseas in Aden at the time. Unknown to both him and the birth mother, their letters to each other were never delivered. The birth mother's father intercepted them because he was employed as a postman in a major mail-sorting centre. This act of censorship resulted in considerable distress for both birth father and birth mother and, according to the birth father, his consequent silence was construed as indifference and this contributed towards the decision to have the baby adopted. Other acts of exclusion were more visible and overt for the other five men in this category: the men who were compulsorily separated from the birth mother either by relatives (usually parents) or welfare workers. One said he felt 'manipulated' by both sets of parents and as a result 'shut everything out'. The other four sought to maintain contact by writing and phoning. In the case of two men, their efforts to see the birth mother and baby resulted in their ejection from the hospital at the time of the birth.

For another ten men their relationship with the birth mother and presence throughout the pregnancy was less subject to external intervention. The relationship with the birth mother continued (and developed in one case) with meetings, weekend contact and correspondence. Two men in this group were married to the birth mother and for them the pregnancy was regarded as a welcome and developmental aspect of the marriage.

Five men's relationship with the birth mother declined and ended after news of the pregnancy (in one case news of the pregnancy was retracted by the birth mother). They had little or no contact with her. In the most extreme case, despite having a steady relationship with the birth mother one man simply fled – from London to Wales. He stayed away for the duration of the pregnancy, the birth and the adoption proceedings. For two men the relationship with the birth mother was already over when they heard news of the pregnancy, however, they became re-involved. One of them re-established a friendship with the birth mother and participated in the adoption arrangements. The other, who was by then involved in home-making with another woman who had become pregnant with his second child, became involved in the adoption process after the first child's birth.

For a large majority of those who provided accounts of the period of the pregnancy (20/28), relationships with the birth mother either continued (ten) or ceased despite their wishes (ten). Contrasts in reactions and behaviour can be seen in the case of the man who ran off, and another man who, on news of the pregnancy, accommodated the birth mother in his room in a shared flat, cared for her and was present at the birth. So the stereotype provided by the man who fled does not hold true for most of the men in the group. The actions of most appear to approximate to that of the behaviour of the second man who provided care and support for his pregnant girl friend. Whilst it should be borne in mind that the men in this study (because they have come forward) were likely to have been committed to their partners and children, such examples of care from the majority of the men stand in contrast to reports of the behaviour of men included in one piece of research on birth mothers. In this, birth mothers reported that over 50 per cent of their male partners abandoned or lost contact with them during pregnancy (Hughes and Logan 1993).

For all of the men in the study, the events and experiences that surround the actual birth of their child further underline the highly charged and complex nature of this pre-adoption period.

The Birth of the Child

Evidence that the majority of the births of the men's children took place in the late 1960s corresponds closely with the peak of all adoptions. The study's pattern of a rise throughout the 1960s and a falling away of numbers is also the case for all adoptions (see Figure 5.2). The majority of births (and therefore experiences) in birth mother studies also show this pattern (Bouchier *et al.* 1991).

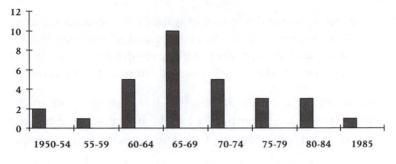

Figure 5.2 Year of Birth of Child (total 30)

Reactions to the News

The majority of the men, who were able to be informed of the birth, reacted to the news with pleasure, delight and a sense of being (pleasantly) overwhelmed, e.g. 'on cloud nine'. Of this group, four referred to pleasure and relief regarding a safe birth and the birth mother's health. One man felt 'gladness and sadness'. Three men expressed a mixture of negative emotions such as guilt and sadness. One felt 'a deep sadness, remorse and guilt'. Two others said that they had felt empty. Two more said that they could not recall how they had responded to news of the birth.

Birth and Fatherhood

Fifteen men saw their children at the time of birth or in the hospital shortly after. They spoke of feelings of pleasure, excitement and pride: 'There was an excitement – this cute wee thing'. Another said that:

> Even although her dad came in and sort of, 'You, boy, out', even with that I still went out of there with a bit of a skip in my step if you like. There was certainly a pride.

A number of men provided specific memories of the child and the time. These are particularly vivid:

> I still say to this day, now and again, I can remember his scent. To me at times it is as if it was only yesterday I can smell him. It's always with me even when I pick up another baby. In my heart I still believe I can still smell his scent sixteen and half years on.

For others the question of adoption lent a jarring note to the event: 'He was lovely, terrific. As I say I felt very, very sad because he was such a lovely looking lad'. Another said of the situation:

> She looked like me. I loved her mum at the time. I think I was trying to distance myself because I knew the adoption was going to happen. That's why I never held the baby.

Five men who had originally had no feelings of fatherhood felt some change:

> I was overwhelmed when I went through to see the baby, in fact massively overwhelmed because this nurse gave me – a just turned 16 year old boy – this tiny little thing that was mine. I can certainly remember being kind of like 'Oh, this is mine'.

One man who did not initially see himself as a father began to experience a change during the pregnancy. His first contact with his child accelerated the growth in his feelings of fatherhood: 'I felt a lump in my throat when I held him. It's quite awe-inspiring what has happened. That hits you more than anything else'. Another man did not welcome the pregnancy, nor did he feel like a father at any time during the pregnancy – he said that he had had a career as rock musician to pursue. At the time of the news of the pregnancy he was in France with a band. However by the time of the birth he had developed strong feelings for the birth mother. He decided to be at the hospital during the birth and afterwards he became involved in caring for the child: 'I went up to the hospital often, held her and helped feed her'.

Twenty-two men were in a position to be involved during this time in that they were in the immediate locality and knew of the impending birth. Of this group 15 attended the hospital, saw, and in some cases, held their child. Therefore a large majority (15/22) chose to have an active involvement in the events surrounding the birth. Eight men expressed a regret at not having been at the birth or at the hospital. The reasons were: being absent in the armed forces (three), the birth mother having been sent to another part of the UK and/or being banned from contact with each other (three). One man was in prison (some months later he saw his son by arrangement with social workers). The eighth man was not wanted at the birth by the birth mother.

Five men appear not to have been committed in so far as they stayed away despite there being no apparent obstacles to their visiting. In practice two appear to have had little motivation by virtue of their having distanced themselves from the birth mother because of new relationships with other women. A third man gave no elaboration as to why his involvement during the pregnancy stopped short of actual attendance during the birth (although in 1963 this was not exactly encouraged). The final two men who could have attended at the birth said that they had decided not to and had rejected any participative role.

For most of the involved men, there was a range of reasons for their participation. Some were there for the birth mother: 'It was my relationship with the birth mother that was the all-pervasive one rather than the relationship with the baby'. Some were pleased that she had had a good birth: 'I was glad it was a good birth, it never gave her any problems'. Some were present at the birth, and some took an active part in feeding and changing the baby: 'I went up often, held her and helped feed her'. For four men, the events around the birth included disputes and fights in the hospital as they sought to have contact with the birth mother and child. For these four, the normally positive experience of visiting mother and new-born baby was marred by the hostility of others and efforts to exclude them.

Harry

Harry was prevented from seeing his child. Anger over this has remained with him since. At the time of the pregnancy he had been going with his girl friend for about a year. He was committed to fatherhood and looking forward to marrying and parenting. The baby's name was chosen by both of them. Two weeks before the birth – the birth mother was only 15, he was 19 – the birth mother's mother intervened and plans were called off.

Harry was looking forward to being able to take the child out and do things: 'I was quite keen.' It was always planned that they would keep the baby, however the birth mother's mother banned her from seeing him. 'She got four guys to give me a doing which did not work because I got the jail for doing them in.' Harry's family knew of the impending birth and his mother had spoken about how they could bring up the child.

Harry went to the hospital when he heard of the birth. There he found out that the birth mother was in labour. Despite being given permission to see her by staff, the birth mother's parents prevented this and there was a fracas and Harry left the building. Shortly after, a friend came out and told him the baby had been born. He did not see the baby then despite wanting to: 'You feel very proud that you are a father.'

The adoption went through. He held John for the first and last time three months later. This was for 30 minutes in the presence of a social worker. 'It still makes me feel angry even thinking back on it.'

One man described an argument at the bedside:

> Karen was sitting bottle feeding Stephen and I said 'Oh great, you're keeping the baby', and she says, 'No, I'm still putting the baby out for adoption'. So we started. I says, 'Why not give the baby to me, to my family?' And she says no. So we had an argument and the Sister came in and grabbed the baby. The way she lifted the baby hurt the baby's neck and I says to the Sister, 'Watch my baby's head'. My voice was probably raised. So I got flung out the hospital.

Half (15) of the entire group did not see the baby, the reasons for which are varied. Six men in this group were unable to do so because they and the birth mother had parted – the responsibility for separation in these cases seems to have been either mutual or at the behest of equal numbers of birth fathers and birth mothers. Five birth fathers were excluded or banned by parents or social workers. Three men were overseas serving in the armed forces. In one case the birth mother was sent away to another part of the country.

Of the 15 birth fathers that never saw the baby, six felt sadness, upset and regret. One man 'didnae have a bond with Lorna because I never even saw her. I always wanted to know what she looked like but I never saw her'. Three could not recall how they felt and had 'shut it out, blanked it'. Two men were reserved and controlled and in the words of one, he was 'frightened to say too much, didn't want to get too involved for fear of opening up again the question of adoption'. In the case of three others who had had no sight of their child, their awareness of the pregnancy and birth was so belated or mediated through official notification that they were unable to comment on their feelings of not seeing the baby. One man presented as one of the most emotionally detached of the group who had not seen their child. In response to whether he had had any sight or touch of the child, he replied:

> I was interested if it was girl or a boy and if she (the birth
> mother) was alright. Frankly I had little experience of what a
> baby might be. I was much more concerned about her.

But this man goes on to say that at the time he was 'sad that there
would be a child who I had fathered who wouldn't know me. Sad,
but in a cool distant way. There was no emotional attachment'.

Eleven men helped name the baby. Of the others, three were
absent in the armed forces and six were prevented from
participation in naming the child as a result of direct exclusion
from the process. Here the actions of external authorities, e.g.
parents and welfare officers begin to assume a high profile in the
narratives and a process of disenfranchisement becomes apparent.
This process is even more emphasised in the numbers involved in
registering the child's birth; just five men were involved in the
official birth registration arrangements. It should be borne in
mind that of these five men two were married to the birth mother.
Ten men did not participate in name-giving. Of these, two men
were actively dissuaded by the birth mother and two knew
nothing of the birth at the time. The other six did not help name
the baby, possibly because they did not see themselves as having
an entitlement to do so (Barber 1975; Connolly 1978; Pannor *et
al.* 1971).

Of the 24 men who could report, four consistently had no
feelings of fatherhood. This leaves a large majority who report
that during this particular period feelings of fatherhood were
present from the beginning or developed in the course of the
events. These 20 men are composed of 12 who had felt like
fathers from the start, three who changed to feeling thus during
the pregnancy and a further five who were so moved as a result of
the birth and sight of their child as to express feelings of
fatherhood.

Of the 30 men in the study as a whole, six could not discuss
their experiences of the pregnancy and birth period. One of these
men did not give an answer (interview conducted by post). One

man said he could not (he was 'unsure' about his feelings towards the child), the other four were not in a position to give a contemporary account of the time because they only found about the pregnancy and the birth some months after. If these six men are deducted from the total it leaves 24 who were able to report on their attitude towards fatherhood during the pregnancy and birth. Four never felt like fathers but 20 men experienced feelings of fatherhood in this period. As noted above in the discussion on feelings during pregnancy, at and after the birth, the men's feelings included pride, ownership, anticipation of a future in which they envisioned themselves as parents of the child-to-be and commitment to home-making plans. The men who felt fatherhood subsequently 'kicking-in', also experienced feelings akin to those of the first group, i.e. ownership ('Oh, this is mine', in the words of one), pride and affection for the child.

An overall summary of the period leading up to and just after the child's birth shows the emergence of certain significant themes.

Summary and Emergent Themes during the Pregnancy and Birth

What can be inferred from the men's accounts of this time? For most, decades after the events of this period (and in one case nearly 50 years on), the effects have resonated and continue to do so in such a way that lends a passion and deep emotional quality to their accounts. The notion of feckless young men who abandon both mother and baby is far from confirmed, even at this early point in their experiences. Three defining features emerge: first, that the time of pregnancy and birth was an extraordinary and impactful life event. Second, that most of the group were involved in events that left them with a substantial sense of loss, and third, that there is evidence of a constellation of feelings and behaviours that indicate the development of a sense of fatherhood.

An Extraordinary Life Event

Most of the men describe the events of this period as having had a considerable and formative impact upon them. A majority were teenagers and very few planned to have a child at that point in their lives. A sense of alarm pervades many of their accounts. The sudden requirement to become more emotionally and socially mature – to consider others such as the birth mother and the unborn child – cut across existing life plans and aspirations. This dual challenge, to become an adult and to become a parent, which faces all young fathers-to-be has been noted elsewhere (Pannor *et al.* 1971). Predictably the birth fathers in this study show a depth and range of emotions that underline the formative and salient nature of this period for them, as for many young fathers.

From first reactions to news of the pregnancy through to the feelings on contact with their baby son or daughter, experiences and feelings were vividly recounted. A similar ability to minutely describe other various events during this period (their whereabouts and actions when first informed of the pregnancy; the detail of certain incidents that took place during the pregnancy and birth; events at the hospital) demonstrates the existence of an enduring set of memories. Yow suggests that: 'if the event or situation was significant to the individual, it will likely be remembered in some detail, especially its associated feelings' (1994, p.19). The fact that a number of men became upset during the interview – 'I was very angry. I felt really angry. It still makes me feel angry even thinking back on it'– underlines the deep impact made on their lives by the experiences of this period.

Another significant factor is the intervention of authority figures. This often took the form of parental pressure to rule out any possibility of the relationship between birth father and birth mother continuing into joint parenting. In three cases statutory welfare services were involved. Strained relationships resulted in irreparable damage to family relations. In other cases the birth father found that his decision-making powers were removed and he was excluded from the pregnancy and birth events. In these instances, most of the pregnancy and birth took place without the participation of the birth father who would have otherwise been involved. These interventions, whether statutory or familial, were experienced as repressive. In other cases Army or Navy strictures produced a similar (imposed) non-involvement and feelings of frustration in the birth father. Such feelings of powerlessness and helplessness left by this set of negative experiences were central to the extraordinary impact of the overall events surrounding the pregnancy and birth.

For all the men who were involved in the birth events – being there at the birth, close by, or present before or shortly after – the birth of their child was a moving and significant event in itself, whether or not they experienced paternal feelings. The sight and feel of their own child deeply affected many of the men as witnessed by their powers of precise recall of its touch and smell. This event was bound up with their feelings of paternity but also for those who had felt no sense of fatherhood throughout the pregnancy and felt none at the birth, the experience was unforgettable and was described in minute and vivid terms.

Loss

The men's narratives begin with the existence of a stable relationship with the birth mother. The pregnancy brings out feelings of fatherhood for many. It is a time of the development and formation of strong bonds either with the birth mother or the baby or both. However it is also a period during which these attachments are severed – resulting in deep feelings of frustration and sadness. A consequence of these separations was that the men involved were not able to see either the birth mother or the child at the time of birth. For some men, although young, certain 'nesting' activities had taken place in a commencement of plans for marriage and a home for their child. Such plans were dismantled as events took a course determined by external pressures. For many these separations left feelings of considerable regret and loss.

The Emergence of Fatherhood

Whether a feeling of fatherhood was present at the beginning of the pregnancy, developed during it or emerged at the birth, by the time of the child's arrival many of the men were feeling and behaving like fathers. The pregnancy was unplanned for the majority of the men and therefore the question of fatherhood was unexpectedly posed to them. As noted, over a third experienced an immediate sense of fatherhood on news of the pregnancy. And by the time of the birth over half of the group had experienced some feelings or thoughts of responsibility towards the child. Some of these feelings took the form of regular and solicitous involvement during labour, the birth and confinement. Other men expressed their hopes of future involvement in play with their son or daughter and others participated in choice of name. Others assumed responsibility for home-making and 'settling down'. In those situations in which the birth father and/or birth mother were under age, discussions took place regarding elopement with a view to living together and raising the child.

Pregnant women may attain the role of mother by automatic ascription although this has been challenged by many writers (e.g. Forna 1998). However unmarried fathers as a whole, whether or not they intend to be involved in keeping the child, are often seen as in a state of suspension pending the hands-on role of parenting a child (Singh and Newburn 2000). However, despite being unable to 'do' fathering (i.e. perform as a father), many of the men in the group felt themselves to have been, and be, a father. Being fathers was expressed in a pride at 'having made a baby', anticipation of future parenting, preparedness for home-making, concern for welfare of the birth mother and unborn child, and a readiness to physically confront individuals and influences that sought to deny them access to and involvement with their new-born child. A feeling of responsibility developed towards the child – the obligation to 'provide a father for her' as voiced by one. These activities and feelings can be said to constitute some of the emotional and psychological dimensions of expectant and new fatherhood in this group of birth fathers.

Whilst a similar range of reactions, feelings, behaviours and aspirations exists in relation to any fathers-to-be who intend to proceed to parent their child, the adoption (and thus separation from the child-to-be) had already begun to loom large for many. Thus the men's narratives had began to depart from those of other more conventional groups of fathers. The break or splitting of the 'father' role into two, the one that they will not become (a social father) and the one that they will remain (a biological father), develops in the next phase: the adoption. However, the germination of a sense of fatherhood and an identity that includes being a father in respect of the child has occurred for a significant number. Therefore, during the period of pregnancy and the birth a distinct birth father 'narrative' begins to emerge.

Thus in these nine months a powerful trinity has formed, consisting of three connected groupings of deeply felt experiences and events: an extraordinary and impactful life event, the experience of loss and the beginnings of feelings of fatherhood. As we shall see, for many of the men, their experiences intensify or commence along these lines.

Chapter Six

The Adoption

It was a very emotional time. It was tinged with great sadness and a certain amount of loss, and anger.

Almost nothing is known about the feelings and behaviour of birth fathers in response to their experiences of the adoption process and proceedings. Only one of the two existing studies of birth fathers discusses their emotions and behaviour during this period (Cicchini 1993). Cicchini found similarities between the experiences of birth fathers and those of birth mothers. Therefore these findings will be a useful reference point in the following discussion.

For many men in the study (17/30) the question of adoption had already been raised prior to the birth of the child. Eight more men were informed at or around the time of the birth in hospital or in the days that followed. Five men remained unaware of the adoption for some considerable time, either months or years. Twenty-five men were then able to report on their involvement in one, some or all aspects of the adoption: the decision-making process, arrangements, leave-taking, legal proceedings – either by choice, reluctantly or in opposition to it. In keeping with the chronological structure, this chapter collates and analyses the feelings, motivations and influences that underlay the men's experiences during the adoption process. Similarly the chapter closes with a summary that seeks to identify some key themes in respect of the adoption of the men's children.

Reasons for the Adoption

The men were asked to discuss who or what lay behind the adoption decision. Intervention by the parents of either the birth mother or the birth father was the greatest reason for the decision to have the child adopted (12/25).

Ian

Ian was an apprentice engineer at the time of his girl friend's pregnancy in 1963. He was 19 and she was 15. They were both shocked by the news: 'immediately filled with dread' – part of which may have been to do with his girl friend's age. They planned on running away but when her parents 'stepped in' Ian said he felt 'a little relief.' The birth mother's parents took the adoption decision: 'This 19 year old boy that had got her pregnant, will we ever see him again? Her mother was out working, the grandmother was working, her father was working, they lived in a tenement, we all didnae have a clue.' The adoption decision seems to have been taken very quickly.

The birth mother was placed in a mother and baby home and when their daughter was born Ian was told of the news by his mother. He did not see his daughter. The birth mother went to the adoption agency twice after she left the home, once with her father and once with Ian to sign 'the final bit of paper.' He waited outside.

A year and half later they married. 'I felt that we got married and we've stuck together because the reward was that she would one day get in touch with us.'

This equates with the birth mother literature (Bouchier *et al.* 1991) in terms of the role of parents in promoting adoption as the only option to teenage pregnancy. It is the parents of the birth mother who feature the most (9/12) in this group of 12 sets of parents. The birth mother's mother was referred to as the driving force in six out of this latter group of nine parents. In only one instance out of these nine sets of birth mother parents was the birth mother's father cited as an active influence in favour of adoption. This bears out findings elsewhere on women's role taking, namely that women are ascribed a central role in relation to emotional and practical responsibility in matters such as these (Rich 1995). The same such role apportionment is echoed in the birth mother literature (Mander 1995). In three cases both sets of parents intervened to ensure that the child would be adopted.

The next most significant reason for the decision to adopt was the decision of the birth mother (4/25). In these cases, the men said that they believed this was because of her career considerations. It was not obvious from the accounts whether there were any other influences in these decisions, i.e. the birth mother's parents or the birth father's unwillingness to proceed with any other alternatives to the adoption. However in two other cases, it was the man's career that was a specific dominant force in favour of the adoption. One of these cases gives a sense of the determination not to parent on the part of the birth father:

> By then (the birth), I had gone up to College and I had shut my mind to the possibility of being married. I had friends and girl friends... I thought quite carefully about it. I thought fairly clinically. Selfishly. I could see my life's prospect and Tim's (a friend who had had to get married after his girl friend had become pregnant). I just knew it was the best thing.

The inability of the relationship to sustain parenting a child was cited by four out of 25 men. The relationship was said to have been brief ('a fling') or not serious: 'We never had that sort of relationship. It would be one mistake compounding another'. In one case the relationship had ended and the father had set up home with another girl who was pregnant with his (second) child.

Reactions to the News of the Decision to Adopt the Child

Whilst 17 men had been informed of or drawn into adoption arrangements prior to the birth, for eight men the news of the adoption of their child came after the birth. The news that their child was to be adopted and plans were in hand had not been anticipated. For most this news was not welcome; three were told in the hospital. In one of these cases the child had had a serious accident in hospital and was, according to hospital staff, brain damaged. Nevertheless, the adoption happened, against the feelings of the birth father. Another two men did not have an ongoing relationship with the birth mother. For these men, the first that they knew of the adoption was when they were informed by the adoption agency. One man was told by the social workers who had brought his child to see him. The seventh and eighth fathers were informed, respectively, by an Army chaplain whilst on service overseas and by prison social workers.

This sudden news of adoption plans added an extra twist to the emotions of the time:

> I felt a lump in my throat when I held him. It's quite awe inspiring what has happened. That hits you more than anything else. While I was standing there holding David, Maureen said that she was having him adopted because that was for the best. I think I said, 'If that's what you want'. I got upset and angry, handed David back and left.

In two cases the relationship had ended; one man had been excluded from the pregnancy and birth events by the birth mother but had hoped to achieve reconciliation – thus the adoption plans were a surprise. In the other case (the man who had set up home and was planning a family with another woman), his reaction to the news of the adoption plans was muted. He felt that he 'shouldn't take a role'.

All of this group of eight men (for whom the adoption plans were not anticipated) were against, or came to oppose, the adoption. Even in the case of the child who had been permanently injured, the birth father felt rushed and had been reluctant to agree the adoption. To a certain extent the disapproval of these men is predictable, given that instead of adoption all but one had envisioned going on to parenting the child. Either they were married to, or had plans to marry the birth mother. A child was seen as logical extension of this relationship.

Arrangements for the Adoption

The adoption cannot be viewed as a single event. In reality the adoption of a child is a process as well as a single act that follows birth. In most cases this process includes a pre-birth period of decision-making that may involve (welcome or not) GPs, social workers and parents, initial contact with adoption agencies, and participation in interviews with adoption practitioners. In the men's accounts, sometimes the adoption was agreed during the pregnancy.

Prior to the birth of their child, over half of the group of men who could report (17/25), said that the question of the baby's adoption had been raised. This involved a variety of types of decision-making, participation or non-participation. Either way, for these 17 men the question of adoption, their attitude to it and potential involvement in plans, were posed before the birth. This took a number of forms and these broadly depended upon whether the birth father was in favour of adoption or not. Eight of the 17 men were more or less in favour of proceeding with the adoption. All but one of this group were involved in the pre-birth adoption arrangements, e.g. meetings with social workers to elicit the views of the birth parents in relation to the upbringing of their child. The one man who was not involved felt he was given no choice: 'No, I can't say the adoption was against my wishes but I really felt that I had no significant choice in the matter'.

This element of 'no choice' is more prevalent amongst those in the group that were opposed to the adoption plans (9/17). The phrases 'no option', 'not consulted' and 'no alternative' feature regularly in their accounts. This was typically expressed as: 'I felt that we, I, had no choice. No option. I felt guilty. The impression was that this was nothing to do with me. I felt isolated'. Often the arrangements, meetings with social workers, completing forms, etc. (because they tended not to include the birth father) produced an additional sense of disenfranchisement. The men affected in this way expressed bitterness and anger over exclusion from discussions about life and family preferences for the child and key matters such as their social and medical profile as a birth parent. However it should be acknowledged that, in all but the recent period, there has been a general practice that tended to discourage unmarried fathers from participation and formal decision--making, e.g. having their names on the child's birth certificate (Anglim 1965; Willmott 1977). At an early stage in the pregnancy, birth and adoption events, it seems then that nine men – a third of the whole group – had felt disenfranchised.

There seems to be a close correspondence between agreement to the plans for adoption and involvement in these and a similar association between opposition to the plans and exclusion from such arrangements.

Involvement in the Adoption Arrangements and Proceedings

Involvement in the adoption is defined here as participation in the adoption process and proceedings. That is, in respect of contributing to arrangements, e.g. communicating preferences for adoptive parents and future lifestyle of the child, sharing personal and family medical histories. Also included are those men who 'participated' by becoming involved in opposition to the adoption plans. The degree of involvement of the 12 men who participated in the adoption process and proceedings ranges from a one-off visit to social workers to regular contact with the adoption agency, and signing consent forms. In at least two cases, men participated in the physical hand-over of their child. In two other cases involvement took the form of opposition (post-birth) to the adoption.

The men attended the various interviews. They supplied details of their religious and schooling preferences for the child, indicated preferences for types of adoptive parent and, when invited to, they expressed their wishes for the child's upbringing, e.g. that the child be encouraged to have an interest in sports. Most of the men – when they were able to be – were supportive and concerned regarding the birth mother's health, feelings and her best interests during the adoption arrangements. It is difficult to say whether the expressions of concern in these reports were derived from a care felt towards the birth mother or towards the child, or both. The reports convey a degree of responsibility as regards the adoption arrangements. It is important to note here (and the point applies elsewhere in the men's accounts) that shifting societal mores may have an effect on how the men tell their stories. For example if the respondents had been interviewed at the beginning of the 1970s instead of the late 1990s, the cultural and societal norms then may have produced less emphasis by the respondents on their notions of responsibility and fatherhood than exists within their narratives today.

The experiences and reasons of the 18 men who were not involved in the adoption proceedings are diverse: six were prevented from playing an active part by external authorities. Five were not aware of the actual adoption proceedings and three were excluded by the birth mother. The other four were, typically, 'not invited in' in the words of one man. Altogether ten of this group of 18 were opposed to the adoption. Being opposed to the adoption was associated with exclusion from the arrangements and, at the least, discouragement from participation. This confirms the US research among birth fathers (Deykin *et al.*

1988). Such exclusion from the process produced anger that often failed to dissipate instead, as will be seen in the reports of the men's lives following the adoption, there were many negative emotions and behaviours provoked by such disenfranchisement.

A total of 23 men – 16 who were against and seven who were broadly in favour of the adoption – were able to talk of their motives and feelings that underlay the adoption decisions.

Feelings during the Adoption Process

Sixteen men were against the adoption. Their feelings here included extreme hostility (4) and distress (4): 'Mentally I didn't want the adoption to happen under any circumstances. I felt that Elspeth was being stolen from me. Someone stole her life away from me.' There was also a sense of powerlessness and the feeling, for six men, that they had no connection with the unfolding events. On receipt of the adoption papers one man felt 'an indignity for what Christine (the birth mother) was going through'. He went on to say that he felt that there was no role for him because the relationship between himself and the birth mother was over. He had also begun a relationship with another woman and expected this to be long term and stable (she was expecting his child). This man's emotional detachment (in terms of what he said regarding his own feelings) changed to opposition to the adoption as the legal proceedings gathered pace:

> I began to feel a growing feeling of responsibility for Linda (his child). She was expecting me to be her father. I decided to oppose the adoption plans. I refused my consent and wrote to the Court to say so. I was prepared to look after Linda.

Two men said that they felt, respectively, 'a sense of relief' and a feeling of 'for the best' in spite of their overall reluctance about the adoption.

Thirteen of the men who opposed the adoption said that they had felt like fathers and/or had feelings of fatherhood at some stage during the pregnancy and birth events. One man said that he had had no feelings of fatherhood, one replied that he was 'unsure' as to his feelings regarding this and the sixteenth man (a postal interview) gave no answer as to his motivation for opposition.

Schwarz (1986) discussed in Menard (1997, p.156) suggests that the motives of birth fathers who oppose the adoption can include pride in paternity or procreation and this may give rise to a view of the child as his or his family's property. Opposition could also stem from a belief held by some birth fathers that history should not be repeated; namely that a child should not be abandoned by their father in the same way that they (the birth fathers to whom this might apply) had been by their fathers. Schwarz also discusses anger at the birth mother as another motive for opposition to the adoption plan. The conclusion is drawn that opposition is 'determined by (the birth father's) feelings about himself, the birth mother and the meaning the adoption has for him'. It is the case that one of the 16 men who expressed their disagreement with the adoption spoke of the child having been 'stolen'. But no man in the study directly associated their opposition to the adoption with any childhood experiences such as loss of their father (I will return to the connection between thoughts of the child and childhood experiences). Only one man talked of his anger at the birth mother but, as in the case of the other 15, he did not officially oppose the adoption. In the case of the motives of the two men who formally objected to the adoption plans there is also little corroboration of Schwarz's suggestions of feelings of the child as property or antagonism towards the birth mother as explanations for their action.

Just as those who were opposed to the adoption experienced a range of emotions from anger to a mix of reluctance and relief, so also was there a similar diversity in the group of seven men who had been in favour. These seven men talked of a range of feelings and behaviour. This includes one man's support for the birth mother that seemed to mask a personal whole-heartedness in support of the adoption, i.e. an expression of agreement by proxy. There were also expressions of qualified agreement accompanied by a mixture of emotions:

> I had no argument with the adoption, it was so inevitable that it would happen although I had reservations about losing contact. We were both very upset at the time; it was becoming final.

Relief was also present: 'We were told that's what was happening and there was an element of a wee bit of semi relief'. Relief plus 'confusion' was felt by another. One man who was 100 per cent in favour of the decision also expressed a mixture of emotions, predominantly in favour of the adoption:

> There was an inevitability. I just wasn't old enough to get married. And I was quite happy with the thing. Except I thought it was sad. Sad that there would be a child who I had fathered who wouldn't know me. But in a very cool distant way.

The accounts of two men show a dissonance regarding their approval and feelings that accompanied this; one was: 'Confused. A traumatic time. It became harder and harder'. The other felt:

> Awful really. Very, very sad. Very mixed feelings. Something I wouldn't have done under any other circumstances. There was high emotions of all sorts. There was so much going on at that period of time. I think I was shell-shocked when I look back. Kind of on auto-pilot.

None of those in favour of the adoption had previously experienced any distinctive feelings of fatherhood except for one man who was definite about feeling like a father. He expressed a sense of ownership towards his child: 'She was my birthday present'. This man had also seen and held his child and his approval of the adoption remains consistent throughout the process and decision-making. His feeling of fatherhood together with a lack of ambivalence regarding the adoption is not typical of the others; he is an exception in the group who endorsed the adoption plans. A remark from one of the others is revealing: 'I was frightened to say too much, didn't want to get involved for fear of re-opening the question of adoption or not'. An apparently pro-adoption attitude may be misleading if it is then assumed that there are no deeper, conflicting emotions and that therefore professional support is not needed. As we shall see, those in agreement with the decision were not exempt from deep feelings of anguish in the days and weeks that followed the adoption.

Two men changed their minds from being for the adoption to being against it. These two men had had no feelings of fatherhood during the pregnancy and birth period. Their decision to contest the adoption and seek to parent their child is worth looking at in greater depth. Both men were 19 years old: one was at university and the other was an apprentice tradesman. The latter saw his child, the other did not. The apprentice withheld his consent for three years whilst financially contributing to his child's maintenance. The student made representations to the court three months after the birth when he decided that the adoption should not go through.

The birth father who was an apprentice at the time had been present in hospital soon after his child was born and had held her. He helped name the baby and, unusually for an unmarried teenage father at that time, his name was used for the registration of the child's name. Events such as this in the period of the birth and immediately after contributed to the conversion of his feelings towards responsibility for his child. It was in hospital that he was informed about the adoption decision; afterwards he and the birth mother (who was underage) drifted apart. The child was placed with foster parents. The father withheld his consent for nearly three years until eventually:

> The only way that I convinced myself (to consent to the adoption) was that she was going to be better off, she's going to have a house, she's going to have clothes. With a more stable family than what she would have with me. I kept hoping that in

those years I'd find somebody that I really want to settle down with. That I could have a mum for her.

When asked what could have been different, this man replied, 'I feel if I had been another five or ten years older, more mature… It's difficult to say. The baby's mum never got married'. In three other cases the men and the birth mother remained together after the adoption and went on to marry. One of these men said they both had continued to regret the adoption for the rest of their lives.

As in the case of the apprentice, the student birth father also converted from having no parental feelings to feeling a similar sense of concern for his child's welfare. This change began during the pregnancy of his second partner. He speculated that his feelings of parental responsibility may have been invoked by the imminence of this second child. He began to feel that the child being adopted needed to have him as her father, that she was demanding this commitment from him. He also spoke of feeling a 'duty of care' and his representations to court included outlining his positive material circumstances, e.g. a stable relationship and an established home. However the adoption went through.

Schwarz's overall conclusion regarding birth fathers' motives for opposition to adoption suggests a combination of the birth father's feelings about himself, about the birth mother and the meaning of the adoption for him. However a significant aspect is missing – the feelings of the birth father towards the child.

Table 6.1 Attitude to adoption and feelings of fatherhood			
	Feelings of fatherhood	*'Unsure' re fatherhood*	*No feelings of fatherhood*
Opposed to the adoption	14	1	1
In favour of the adoption	1	0	6

Those men who felt like fathers during the pregnancy and birth period (or later came to feel thus as in the case of the two men previously discussed) were much more likely to be amongst the ones who actively opposed the adoption. And those who did not feel like fathers were those who were broadly in favour of the adoption. This must be of interest to social workers who may be confronted with the difficult problem of whether or not to include an angry (oppositional) birth father in the adoption plans. Any opposition may become more acute the less a birth father perceives that he is included, that his sense of fatherhood has not been acknowledged. This is of no help in the proceedings or in later life when it may appear to the child that its father was absent from such a crucial decision-making process.

Giving up the Child

Altogether 15 men were involved in either the act of giving their legal consent to the adoption, physically leaving the child, or both.

Leave Taking (15 men)

These acts were painful experiences, particularly felt by the seven men who were involved in physically leaving their child – either at the hospital or at the house of foster parents or by handing him or her over to welfare workers:

> I was there when Maureen had to leave from the hospital. Her mother and father were there. It was just like getting ready for going home, like a normal mother would do, getting her stuff together, getting the baby ready. Then the social worker come and took the baby. I'm not sure if I imagine this but I actually saw her putting the baby in the car and driving off. We all had a cuddle of her anyway. You know what I mean. That was the bad moment. I was cuddling Diane (birth mother), probably restraining her as well really.

For one man taking his good-byes was a protracted 'trauma' caused by increasingly tense visits, spread over six months, whilst their child remained in foster care awaiting adoption.

Eleven of this group were asked to sign their consent to the adoption: eight men signed and three refused. Of those who refused to sign their consent, two became involved in formal challenges to the proceedings and the third eventually signed after three years. Two of these three men (who refused their consent) had had feelings of fatherhood and a desire for a family. I have discussed these two men above: the apprentice/birth father who eventually signed his consent to the adoption and the student/birth father whose consent was dispensed with (his opposition 'noted' in the court letter that he brought to the interview). In the case of the third man who withheld his consent, he asked and was permitted to attend court on the day of the adoption proceedings 'to put my point forward'. He did this not so much to offer an alternative to the adoption plans – by this time he was married to another woman who was (mentally) 'not well', living in a one-bedroom flat and had no job stability – but it seems, to have his day in court. By the time of the court hearing he understood that the adoption was inevitable yet he said he felt that he needed to be recorded as having been a party to the proceedings.

This man's attitude was tinged with 'bitterness' and an anger that was present during his account. He had been excluded from all events except the early part of the pregnancy, e.g. he was notified of the birth of his child, her sex, weight, etc. by the adoption agency a week after the event. At the court his contribution was noted for the record, he refused to sign his consent and after the proceedings (which resulted in approval of the adoption) he departed but 'felt a bit better'. When asked whether he had had feelings of fatherhood during this period, he was 'unsure'.

Signatures of consent to the adoptions did not necessarily mean agreement with the events or an absence of any feelings of fatherhood. All of the eight men who signed experienced feelings of fatherhood and a wish to make a family. However, by the time of the consent to adopt – in most cases some months after the birth – the adoption was felt to be inevitable.

Those Who Did Not or Could Not Participate in Giving up the Child (15)

Six men were absent or unaware of the adoption at the time and had no option about involvement or otherwise. This leaves another nine men who, despite being present at the time of the adoption, neither physically nor legally participated in any leave taking concerning their child.

Six of these nine men had been excluded from the adoption process and proceedings. Of the remaining three men, the report of one remains consistent with his description of himself as having 'no emotional attachment'; he agreed to the adoption, had no involvement in the arrangements and took no part in any giving up of the child. Neither did he see the child. The birth mother had been sent to Scotland to live with relatives and it was there that the baby was born and adopted. The two other men were both, in their different ways, committed to the adoption plan. Both were involved in attending interviews during the adoption process. One 'did not feel like a father' during this period but began to feel some curiosity as to how his child would develop. He also began to have reservations about losing contact with him. He elected not to see his child in hospital because as noted his actions might 're-open the question'. It seems fair to suggest that this man, by not looking at his child, was seeking to avoid the possibility of changing his mind and wishing to call off the adoption. The third man had had feelings of fatherhood during the pregnancy and had seen his child in hospital.

There is therefore only one man who felt like a father, was committed to the adoption of his child and took part in arrangements. Unlike the vast majority of the others this man had had four other children prior to the child that was given up for adoption (he was 32 when he and the birth mother began their relationship). His account raised the question of whether there was difference between men who were first-time fathers-to-be, their feelings of fatherhood and their attitude to adoption and the attitudes of men for whom the child to be adopted was not their first. The question needs more extensive research with a larger sample, however two other men in the study had previously had children from their marriage to the birth mother of the child and these two were engaged in parenting their children when the second child was adopted. The decision to have this child adopted was a difficult decision for them. It was against their wishes. In these two cases experience of already having been a father did not seem to make the adoption decision any more predictable or easy.

The Formal Consent

Twenty-three men were theoretically in a position to sign their formal consent to the adoption, i.e. they were either immediately on hand or could be contacted by the authorities. In the case of the other seven men, five were uncontactable and two, by this time, had been excluded by the birth mother. Of the 23 contactable men, nine were not offered the opportunity to sign. Nine did sign their consent (although one man took three years to bring himself to do so), two refused to provide their formal consent, and three men could not remember whether they did or did not. If the two married men are deducted this leaves a high number (7/20) of unmarried men (mostly teenagers) who were offered such an option in relation to the legal process of the adoption of their child. This is high in terms of the then general practice of not actively inviting young teenage fathers to take part in similar official proceedings such as birth registration (Platts 1968; Willmott 1977).

The level of involvement, from physical relinquishment to official signing of consent to adopt; the number in the group who participated in the process and the degree to which some of them were involved, provides some qualitative evidence of unmarried teenage fathers' willingness to be involved in adoption decision-making. More specifically, the reports of the men in this matter (whether involved or prevented from involvement) do not confirm the suggestion that birth fathers tend not to be involved in the adoption process (Lightman and Schlesinger 1982; Mander 1995). When invited and encouraged, it would seem that more birth fathers than at present would participate in the decision-making and (if adoption is agreed) the arrangements process.

The above discussion has taken events up to and including the final physical and legal disconnection between the men and their children. What were the after-effects of this?

Feelings Following the Adoption

In keeping with previous research relating to birth mothers (Winkler and van Keppel 1984) and the Australian study of birth fathers (Cicchini 1993), the men were invited to talk about their feelings in the weeks and months immediately following the adoption. Twenty-six men contributed to most of the following discussions: the other four men found out about the adoption more than a year afterward and therefore could not substantially discuss the immediate post-adoption period.

Little or No Effects

For five men the adoption had little or no immediate effect, although they acknowledged an element of denial to varying degrees. One said that whilst he had felt that his child was being 'stolen' from him during the adoption process, afterwards 'it wasn't a major problem' (the rest of this man's account reveals that three years on 'things begin to grate'). A second man indicated the impact less directly, saying that the adoption had had no effect on him because:

> I shut it out. I literally put it behind me. I'd never known anyone in that situation before. There had always been kids around. It (having children) was a natural thing. But it was always there.

His declaration that he was not affected by the adoption is somewhat belied by this quote.

Three other men were less ambiguous in their responses as to whether or not they had experienced any after-effects relating to the adoption. One man had had no feelings afterwards because he had begun parenting a step-daughter (from another relationship) who served as 'a substitute' for the daughter that had been adopted. The second's account was consistent with his feelings throughout the process: he had had 'no emotional connection' with the event and had known that it was the best thing to do. This man had felt 'nothing' after the adoption. The third 'wondered what had happened' to his child in the weeks and months after her adoption. During the interview this man presented as the one who was the most matter-of-fact in relation to his overall experiences. He was also the least forthcoming. He is the one in the group who was much older than the rest at the time of the adoption and who had previously parented four children.

Negative After-effects

A large majority (21/26) experienced emotional discomfort or distress after the adoption. There are reports of depression and self-harm, and ill-judged decisions to enter into marriage. Although the tendency was for the majority to report what were felt to have been powerful negative reactions, the accounts of four of this group were somewhat less powerful. One man said that he had felt 'a bit upset', another felt 'occasional guilt' and one other said that at the time he was:

> ... too young to have the kind of feelings that someone maybe two or three years older would have had and I had that

immatureness, if you like, in me that I was still a young lad (16). I felt a certain loss in that he was gone and I would never see him.

If these four relatively less powerful accounts are removed from the number of those who had experiences of emotional turbulence there remain 17 accounts of discomfort, distress, dysfunctional behaviour[1] or all three. The reports range from, in the case of one man, feelings of despair that resulted in attempted suicide and another who mentioned feeling suicidal and being 'very depressed', to men who said that in the months after the adoption they typically felt 'numb', 'manic' or 'very upset'. One man's response to the question contains feelings that recur in many of the accounts:

> I became a very angry person after she was born. I used to go to dance halls looking for trouble. I just turned violent for a long time. I used to go out with quite a few guys. We used to get into trouble. Just being stupid. Hitting other people. I turned to drink some times. A couple of times I tried drugs.

> I was having trouble sleeping. I was having back pain. I wasn't mentally ill but I ended up at the Andrew Duncan (a local psychiatric hospital) as an outpatient. What I was doing was punishing myself. I was trying to punish myself for what I had done.

The mildest of these reports describes being 'worried' about the child and having many anxieties.

One man became 'very depressed, it was a lonely time, I could have committed suicide'. Others said that they had 'lost of part of (me)', it was 'like a bereavement', and during this 'traumatic

---

1 'Dysfunctional behaviour' includes either that of an uncharacteristic and explicit anti-social nature, e.g. arrestable activity such as violence to others, or personal abuse such as extended drinking bouts and illegal drug taking.

period' they felt 'anguish'. Turning their feelings inwards left its mark. Three men made unhappy marriages – one of them used the term 'on the rebound' to describe his reasons for marrying soon after the adoption. Three others talked of irreparable rows with their mothers and permanent departure from their homes. These disrupted relationships were said to be a result, direct or indirect, of the adoption. One man dropped out of college as a result of his distress. Two men said that the turbulence of their post-adoption feelings was resolved in a particular choice of career; one became a social worker with children. The case of birth fathers who, in later life, become employed in the child care field has been identified by others (e.g. Rosenberg 1992, p.39).

For a majority then, in very practical terms (criminality, relationships and careers), the consequences of the adoption of their child were far-reaching within 12 months. The cause of such serious turbulence is worth exploring and it is helpful to ask if the degree of distress has a relation to three factors. The first is concerned with opposition to or agreement with the adoption. Is it the case that opposition to the adoption equates with a greater negative reaction? In other words, did agreement with the adoption mean less of an extreme post-adoption reaction?

Those Who Agreed with the Adoption

It appears that agreement with the adoption did not make the weeks and months after less turbulent. Of the seven men who were in agreement with the adoption at the time, two reported virtually no effect on their lives in the months following the adoption. One of these two men felt some curiosity. The second experienced 'occasional guilt' afterwards. However, of the other five, one man described the period as: 'a mixed emotional time – feeling bad and a lot of self-interest'. Other experiences ranged from feelings of confusion and a row with the birth mother on the first anniversary of the birth of the child, to more extreme accounts of 'lots of difficulties' and a marriage entered into 'on the rebound'.

Amongst those who agreed with the adoption, a majority (5/7) experienced negative after-effects. This is surprising – on the presumption that agreement to the adoption ought to have indicated a positive attitude that would in turn have helped dilute more extreme reactions. Therefore an association between agreement and fewer after-effects is not in evidence. It may be then that an evaluation of the after-effects of the adoption can be too narrowly focused upon the agreement or disagreement decision. In the case of five men, it appears that negative after-effects may also be to do with the experiences and events *throughout* the overall process from pregnancy to adoption.

Those Who Disagreed with the Adoption

Seventeen men were able to discuss both their disagreement and the adoption's effects on them. Was there more turbulence in their lives immediately after the adoption than in the case of those who agreed? The convention that holds that there is an association between adjustment to decisions depending upon agreement or opposition applies better in the case of those who were anti-adoption. The behaviour and reports of 16 of the men who were against the adoption indicate considerable post-adoption distress. Only one man of this group of 17 was unaffected afterwards: 'It wasn't a major problem straight after the adoption'. In other words, this study has found that disagreement with the adoption and negative after-effects are related.

However an unexpected finding has also emerged. After analysis of the reactions of the group who discussed their agreement or disagreement with the adoption, negative reactions to the adoption could not have been forecast on the presumption that only those who disagreed with the decision would experience distress. A majority of those who were in favour of the adoption also experienced distress in the weeks and months afterwards. The figures are too small to draw any general conclusions, however it may be speculated that the adoption of a child is a distressing act and process irrespective of whether there is agreement. What about the level of involvement in the adoption process and proceedings and the degree of distress? In other words, did participation in decision-making cause less of a negative reaction in the weeks and months that followed the adoption?

Relationship between Participation in the Adoption and Degree of After-effects

Those men who participated in the adoption process and plans were just as likely to have experienced emotional turbulence as those who did not. Indeed the ideal configuration (in terms of imagined adjustment) of support for the adoption plus involvement in the arrangements was in place in the cases of six men. Yet five of this group of six underwent post-adoption distress. This ranged from 'anguish' to the account of one man who 'lost all sense of direction and meaning to life'. The man who was the father of four previous children is the sixth man. He agreed with the adoption and participated in arrangements and said that he had felt no discomfort afterwards. Overall (albeit in respect of a numerically small group), there seems to be a lack of relationship between participation or not and whether or not the men felt distress immediately after the adoption.

Table 6.2 Relationship between participation in adoption arrangements and later distress		
	Distress	*Little or no distress*
Participated in adoption arrangements	11	1
Did not or could not participate in arrangements	10	2

Any notion that participation in the adoption process may have eased an adverse emotional reaction is not borne out by the men's accounts. It appears that the men who felt most like fathers were the ones who underwent the most distress,but notwithstanding this a majority of the group experienced some form of emotional upset after the adoption. Did those who felt like fathers feel worse than those who did not?

Relationship between Feelings or not of Fatherhood and the After-effects of the Adoption

The men reported that the time taken to reach calmer emotional waters ranged from a minimum of 18 months to five years. An eventual change in feelings of distress took place for 16 men. Of this group, nine had had some feelings of fatherhood and seven said that they had not. In the case of the seven men whose feelings did not change, five of them (5/7) had experienced feelings of fatherhood, one did not and one man was unsure as to having had any feelings of fatherhood at the time.

Comparing these two groups cannot be done in any quantitative sense. However, there is an indication that feelings of fatherhood are proportionally more likely to appear in the group of men who experienced negative after-effects in relation to the adoption. Or put another way, in the group of men that felt pain and distress after the adoption, there were more who felt like fathers than in the group for whom there were no such negative after-effects. Feelings of fatherhood may then have played some part in the distress during this period. To remain with the question of the part played by feelings of fatherhood, two additional questions are posed here.

First, does the *time* taken for distress to subside bear any relation to whether or not any of them had felt like fathers? The time taken to arrive at a measure of stability seems to bear no relationship to whether or not a man had had feelings of fatherhood, e.g. one who had had distinct feelings of fatherhood took 18 months to settle down after the adoption. For him it was 'a long time to be angry'. Conversely, another who did not report paternal feelings took five years to adjust to the negative effects of his experience.

Second, if distress exists across the group, does the *depth* of this distress have a relationship to whether or not the men experienced feelings of fatherhood? Nine men said that they underwent serious distress after the adoption, including self-harm and receiving clinical treatment for depression. Seven of the men had feelings of fatherhood and two said that they had had none. However, the converse points to a stronger suggestion. Of 12 men whose post-adoption experiences were that of distress but not as outwardly extreme as the others (being 'upset', feeling 'bad' and experiencing 'a mixed time'), more of this group had little or no feelings of fatherhood: 8/12. So whilst nearly all of the men experienced levels of distress after the adoption, the depth of emotional turbulence is associated with whether or not they felt like fathers. In other words, those men who felt little or no sense of fatherhood were likely to be among those who had somewhat less of a difficult emotional time after the adoption. The birth mother research does not enquire into an association between feelings of motherhood and the strength of post-adoption after-effects, presuming as it seems to do, that the women would have felt like mothers. Nevertheless, adverse reactions in the months that followed fall on both sides of a line dividing supporters and opponents of the adoption. If adoption is understood as a process (for birth fathers as well as birth mothers), rather than an event, and agreement and participation not necessarily indicative of a lack of distress, then this suggests that birth fathers also must be targeted for support and counselling in their own right.

Whether the experiences of the men included behaviour and emotions that subsided, intensified or were relatively insignificant during the adoption events, they took place in a social context. Other people played a part in either the amelioration of distress – or its intensification.

Social Influences During the Adoption Process

Apart from the birth mother there were other people who played significant roles during this time, principally parents (both sets) and welfare workers. At various points the actions of these people were influential, e.g. in confirming a sense of exclusion, by defraying some of the distress or through a denial of this distress with either an exhortation 'to get on with life' or hostility.

Parents

The 12 instances in which parents intervened in favour of the adoption have been discussed. The birth mothers' parents were the prime movers in nine of these cases. In at least two other adoptions both sets of parents were instrumental in the adoption decision. This went to the lengths of the two pairs of parents organising living accommodation for the pregnant birth mother at the home of the birth father's parents whilst the birth father was sent to another part of the country. These parents of the birth mother and the birth father then ensured that the teenagers had no contact with each other and initiated adoption plans. More frequent than such concord between both sets of parents were reports of offers by the parents of the birth father to assist in raising the child.

In three cases the birth father said that his parents had made explicit offers to care for the child. One of these offers was declined by the birth father because it was conditional on the child being raised as that of his parents, i.e. as his sister and he foresaw a time when he would not be able to endure such a deception. In the three other cases the offers of the birth father's parents were ignored by adoption workers. In an additional three other cases, the birth father's parents were opposed to the adoption plans. In one of these, the birth father's request that his parents be approached went unheeded by prison welfare officers. The relative lack of status that pertained, e.g. there being no legal locus for the birth father, would seem to have had its effect on the wishes of both the birth father and his family.

In five cases there was no active intervention or offers from either set of parents. In two of these cases, the birth father and birth mother were older than the others and therefore, probably, the adoption events were without the knowledge of their parents.

Welfare Workers

Welfare workers were also influential. One man felt they had been helpful in that he had felt included in consultations and the decision-making process. Otherwise the activity and attitudes of welfare personnel came in for criticism: 'didn't think they did enough to talk us out of it', while hospital staff made one man '...feel neglected. Forgotten about' and another man was ordered to leave the bedside. For one, they were:

> ... biased and biased and biased, she (the social worker) was in favour of the adoption. No matter what you asked her it was always 'in the long term he will go to a good home. He will be brought up by good parents'. What right did she have saying that? I am a good parent.

Another social worker was '...a bit abrupt with me. She said "Father or no father, you do not have any rights as to whether the adoption goes through".' One man travelled to Cork from Scotland to place his child with nuns who were to arrange the adoption. When he and the birth mother arrived at the gates of the convent in Ireland:

> It was very short. It was extremely business-like. No small talk at all. It wasn't pleasant. There was certainly no hospitality. Dare I say there was (sic) possibly feelings of disapproval – two healthy people giving up a baby? I felt awful, dreadful.

The final section of this chapter draws together some threads that have emerged in this discussion of the adoption and the 12 months after. Some interpretation is offered of the themes of distress and loss and fatherhood that have begun to emerge.

Emergent Themes during the Adoption – Grief, Distress and Powerlessness and Fatherhood Interrupted

Whilst the self-selected nature of the group needs to be borne in mind there is a very large majority of the men in the group who had adverse reactions in the weeks and months after the adoption had been finalised. These reactions appear whatever the stance taken on the adoption. Both the groups of men – those who were broadly for the adoption and those who were against it – reported emotional turbulence. Why are there 21 reports out of 25 that speak of distress at this time? Was it a 'period of crisis'? (Cicchini 1993, p.10) Whatever the final outcome in terms of opposition or approval, participation or not, their distress levels after the adoption and whether or not the men experienced feelings of fatherhood, for most, the adoption process was emotionally taxing. The process and proceedings of the adoption, requirements for decision-making, whether he was to be (could be) present or absent during the process, the questions as to his commitment to the relationship, the leave-taking (legal and physical) of the child, were all factors that produced an intensity of emotions.

Some important parallels between the experiences of birth mothers and those of the men in this study can now be drawn. Descriptions of adverse after-effects in the research amongst birth mothers' immediate post-adoption feelings are echoed in the reports of the men. Bouchier et al. (1991, p.50) found 'sadness and loss' and list anger and resentment, inadequacy and frustration, isolation and rejection, guilt or shame, and fear of the future and anxiety about the child amongst the feelings of birth mothers in the months after the adoption. Three accounts, one from Bouchier et al. and two from the men in this study, show similarities between the immediate post-adoption experiences of birth mothers and birth fathers with the expression of anger towards self and others:

I drifted further and further from my own family, rejecting them as they had done me. I lost my self-respect and this led to a lack of control, forethought and direction. Drugs, drink and promiscuity were the result. I became unable to trust adults and made myself thoroughly objectionable and argumentative. Eventually I became very depressed and tried to kill myself by taking an overdose. (Bouchier *et al.* 1991, pp. 53–54)

I left my parents' house. And got lost for a wee while. I drank a lot. Buried my head in the sand. Then it was a lot of bitterness and angerness and a bit like a bereavement.

I lost all sense of direction and meaning to life, ran wild, lost my self-esteem.

Other activities, e.g. self-abusive behaviour such as drinking, drugs binges and overdoses seem common to both sets of experiences. A repeated theme is that of painful reactions in the weeks and months following the adoption. These similarities between the experiences of birth fathers and birth mothers confirm the findings of the only other study to inquire into birth fathers' emotional responses to the adoption (Cicchini 1993).

Grief Reaction

An important conclusion in the birth mother research (Brodzinsky 1990) and that of Cicchini is that in the birth parent emotions and behaviour after adoption there can be found a 'grief reaction'. This also emerged in this study. A number of the men compared their emotional reaction to the adoption to their response to a loved one's death. They referred to their feelings regarding the adoption as 'up there' or comparable with the effects of such deaths. Death and bereavement were used as yardsticks with which to measure their feelings regarding having given up a child for adoption. Others reported that their experience of the adoption was worse because, whereas feelings of loss concerning the death of a loved one could include a sense of finality, the adoption experience lacked such an eventual resolution. This was because the child who had been 'lost' as a result of the adoption was still in existence. One man expressed this succinctly and captured the feelings of others when he said about his father's death:

> That hurt. But you know that's something that's dead, it's gone. I think it's worse when it's something that's gone but you know is alive, and hopefully well somewhere. I think that's harder to cope with than someone who has a bereavement or loses a baby. That's sad, but that's something that goes away, you live with it, you cope with it. You don't walk down the street and turn round a corner and see a young girl and think 'I wonder', 'could be'.

How does this compare with birth mothers' feelings of grief? Research has found unresolved grief in birth mothers' emotional and psychological lives after the adoption of the child. This is likened to bereavement (Bouchier *et al.* 1991; Brinich 1990) and to feelings following peri-natal death (Winkler and van Keppel 1984).

Millen and Roll suggest that the experiences of birth mothers not only conform closely to Parkes' (1972) features of conventional grief but that, in addition, the special nature of such experiences fulfil the conditions that would constitute a state of 'pathological grief' (1985). The emotions, behaviour and feelings reported by some of the birth fathers in this study correspond with aspects of Parkes' taxonomy, and also include pathological grief. For instance, many of the men talked of loss. In at least three cases they likened this to a bereavement, with the added complexity (echoing the finding of Millen and Roll) that for them the child lived on. The inability to settle, anti-social behaviour and drinking bouts also correspond with the second feature of Parkes' paradigm of grief reaction – feelings of being panicky, irritable, tense, jumpy, and in a turmoil – or what he called 'restless anxiety' (quoted in *ibid.* p.413).

A third component in the normal grief reaction is termed 'searching'. Millen and Roll refer to a woman who had given up a child six years previously and continued to be startled by any child whom she thought looked like her child. They show a 'fit' between the searching aspect of grief reaction and the feelings and activities of the birth mothers in their study. Millen and Roll suggest that, uniquely in the case of birth mothers, searching may not be futile. This searching phenomenon is also present in the behaviour of some of the men years after the adoption. In the case of a few, such behaviour is present in the months immediately following the adoption.

A fourth aspect of grief reaction is that of anger and guilt and again there are parallels between what some of the men report regarding their feelings of bitterness and self-blame. According to Millen and Roll, unlike the notion of a conventional grief reaction that involves the eventual subsidence of anger directed towards others, the bitterness of most of the birth mothers in their study appeared to intensify. This is because third parties (e.g. social workers and parents) were felt to have been coercive or cruel. Yet again there are similar feelings in the men's reports, e.g. no levelling off of their adverse and negative emotions. Birth mothers in the Millen and Roll study also talked of feelings of physical loss of self. Again some men in this study felt the same way; one felt he had: 'lost part of me'.

Identification is seen as another component of grief reaction. Here there is somewhat less congruence between the findings of Millen and Roll and the men in this study. Millen and Roll suggest that identification or a lack of a sense of separateness in the birth mother experiences is made complex by the physical reality of pregnancy (Parkes uses the example of identification with the loved one by a bereaved person). The experience of pregnancy may intensify the feeling of oneness with the lost person/child who was adopted. Obviously, none of the men in the study could report such feelings therefore nothing in their accounts relates to this aspect of grief reaction.

The seventh and final feature of grief reaction is termed pathological grief or, in Parkes' phrase, 'atypical grief'. This is the presence of features that prolong or delay the conventional mourning process. Millen and Roll point to such detrimental features for birth mothers in their study as: the social stigma involved in the adoption of a child; external events that prevent the adequate expression of feelings of loss; an uncertainty as to whether or not there is actual loss; an absence of mourning at the relevant time, and the lack of mourning rituals. There is evidence for all of these features in the men's accounts. One man's experience encompassed all of these factors. He was subject to social stigmatisation as a result of his sexual relationship with the birth mother. There was an absence of sympathetic personnel in the detention centre where he then lived and this prevented any discussion of his feelings of being apart from his girlfriend during the birth. He had to be 'tough' for both of them at the point at which the child was physically removed from them. Following this emotional leave-taking he had to return to the detention centre and behave as if nothing had happened.[2] There are some echoes of this experience in the accounts of other men – one was in prison during most of the pregnancy and the birth, and another was in the army at the time of the birth. Neither of these men was able to voice any feelings of loss.

Thus in these feelings, behaviours and experiences there are parallels with what birth mothers may go through: a pathological grief reaction born of a sense of loss. Additionally, such a reaction is deepened by the experience of the unique event of the adoption in which loss does not equate with conventional instances such as bereavement. In adoption the child is 'lost' yet lives on. Another area of similarities in the accounts of these birth fathers and those of birth mothers is that of feelings of distress and powerlessness.

---

2 In March 2000 Martin committed suicide. His partner attributed this to his unresolved feelings of loss and grief.

Distress and Powerlessness

The finding that the men went through periods of upset and emotional turbulence whether or not they agreed with the adoption and irrespective of their exclusion from or inclusion in the events, are based upon too small a group to draw conclusions. However the presence of distress throughout is interesting. This is so especially given that Cicchini (1993) suggests that a lack of participation in the process may ensure the continuation of negative after-effects for birth fathers. Sachdev (1991) also suggests that greater involvement by birth fathers in the adoption decision may contribute to an increase in positive feelings concerning the adoption. Research in other fields allows a wider comparison. Here there is a conventional belief that participation in potentially distressful situations aids recovery. For example, attendance at the funeral assists the bereaved one in dealing with their distress. In a study of parental involvement in medical decision-making regarding the withdrawal of treatment to an ill child, McHaffie and Fowlie suggest that emotional and mental health is strengthened if there has been parental participation (1996, pp.182–183). The same point about the therapeutic benefits of service user involvement in decision-making during admission to residential care is also made by Brearley *et al.* (1980). Yet this study has found something different. Findings of distress felt by many of the men after participation in the adoption arrangements do not support the idea that involvement in a potentially distressing process assists the person in their ability to recover from any of its negative after-effects. These findings and the related other (that agreement with adoption is not a predictor of better adjustment) are interesting as they appear to go against the flow of other research results. However, it should be borne in mind that in this study, it is the immediate short-term effects, i.e. under 12 months, which are under discussion.

Feelings of powerlessness, whether occurring for the first time during the adoption or as a continuation of a process that began during the pregnancy, were also present. The adoption phase continued a process of disenfranchisement that had already begun. In many cases the two periods overlap because adoption arrangements were set in train during the pregnancy. This cumulative process was characterised by experiences of either being offered no choice, the removal of choice or having been actively disbarred from the unfolding events of birth and adoption. Such experiences produced anger and guilt at having been unable to affect what felt like an inexorable and painful process. There were powerful and disturbing memories: 'We were given no options', 'I hated the hospital for that', 'I was angry. Really, really angry. Still am'. Such feelings of disempowerment intensified (or for some, began) during the period of the adoption process and proceedings. For some men, exclusion took a concrete form in moves to prevent them from participating in official decision-making.

Taken together the distress and powerlessness experienced by the men in the group need to be seen in a wider context than just that of the adoption. The effects of the entire sequence of events – from awareness of pregnancy through the birth to their child's adoption – on such young men cannot be underestimated. By the time they had reached 12 months after the adoption many of them had gone through a considerable flux of emotions: 'high emotions of all sorts', an 'emotional roller-coaster'.

Fatherhood Interrrupted

This then was a time of extreme emotions for which there was no relief or outlet. The 'natural order' of things for many of the men, when faced with the situation of their girlfriend's pregnancy, was to foresee some form of family life and parenting; yet this was problematic for them. But even those who had debated then rejected the idea of becoming a parent experienced distress, possibly arising from having had some form of contact with their child, possibly because they went through a separation from the birth mother, perhaps both. In two cases, the men said that their initial rejection of parenthood altered. They 'converted' from feeling no sense of paternal obligation to, as one man put it, a belief in their 'duty of care'. Both of these men resisted the adoption (unsuccessfully) on the basis that they wished to provide a family for their child.

An evaluation of these narratives up to this point suggests the existence of a considerable degree of energy (particularly psychological and emotional) and drive as the pregnancy and birth is followed by the adoption process. For most of the men the onward movement of these powerful emotions was not arrested by the fact of the adoption. There was no resolution except in the negative – the focus (their child) was removed. In the words of one man: 'The adoption rubbed me out legally but not emotionally'. This comment echoes that of Millen and Roll who remark: 'The maternal experience does not end with the signing of the surrender papers' (1985, p.411). Some men specifically recalled frustrated paternal feelings. During the months following the adoption one man was 'very upset at losing (my) daughter' while another:

> ... felt disappointed and a bit upset. Because now I was going to have to face the next seventeen years – minimum – without having to see anything or knowing about Eileen. It might seem a very strange thing being (only) a bit upset but that's the reality. I had already resigned myself to losing her.

What alters now is that during the pregnancy the birth mother and the child within her form one corporeal centre of attention and interest. At its birth, the child becomes a physical reality: a he or a she. Some of the men were involved in naming the child; baby clothes for the right gender were bought. Some of them held their child while others fed their son or daughter. For some men, their fatherhood now had a living and breathing manifestation. In the light of this, it is not surprising that by the time of the adoption, the overall number of men who reported feelings of fatherhood had increased. Yet with the act of adoption this focus of their attention ceases to be. Whether as planned in the months or days before the birth, at the birth or shortly afterwards, the adoption decision went through and their child was gone. Within a very short time the child in their lives came and went. Sometimes this was experienced as a physical process; the child was seen, held and handed over. In other cases it took the form of a series of official and legal events as the fathers attended interviews and participated in giving official consent. For some, both processes were at work – the physical and the official.

In three cases the adoption process and proceedings were drawn out. Consider, for example, the man who did not wish to parent his child but who became involved in protracted (and increasingly painful) visits to the foster parents who were looking after his daughter pending the adoption. For most, however, once the papers had been signed or the final leave-taking had occurred, there was no more focus. Even the two or three men who had consistently felt detached from the process and could report no sense of fatherhood or connection with the child talked of disquiet in the immediate post-adoption months. In the light of the comment by Weiss that 'adults may in a very brief time develop very strong investment in newly born children' (1991, p.74), the men's distress is not surprising.

The end of the formal adoption proceedings with its connotations of finality lends an emotional salience to this period. The legal 'full stop' placed after the adoption produced powerful feelings. There was no sense of 'closure' yet emotions were running high. Feelings appear to have reached an impasse as regards the possibility of a positive outcome. Instead such frustration and bitterness is later expressed in a variety of harmful and adverse ways. If the first 12 months after the adoption were a period of emotional turbulence and distress, what of the men's lives in the years after – did time heal?

Chapter Seven

Life After Adoption

A secret set of emotions.

This chapter continues the men's narratives from 12 months after the adoption up to the point where most decided that they wanted contact with their (adult) child. It is impossible to provide a comprehensive account of the subsequent lives of the men in the group. Many other things had happened to them: at least three of the men suffered the deaths of other children in the years following the adoption. Others had their next child or children and parented them. Some men lost their parents. Some had strokes, others had risen to be high in their professions and others were facing redundancy. Yet as we will see the adoption and their child were unforgettable.

The men were asked to cast their minds back and talk their way through experiences and events that were some 30 years in the past. However, as their accounts approached the present day, the information on relationships with the birth mother and other adults, parenting, where the adoption fitted in their lives, thoughts of the child, began to be affected by two factors. These were: first, whether the men were now in contact with their child and, if so, how this was going (one man who had been contacted by his adopted daughter rated the adoption experience as the most profound in his life). He explained that this might not have been the case a year prior to our interview because then relations with his (newly contacted) daughter had been traumatic and painful. Additionally, whilst one man was recalling events that took place 11 years ago, 47 years had passed for another. Overall there was an average of 28 years between the adoption of the child and the interview.

With such considerations of possible bias (good experience of contact might lend a rosier glow to the account) and recall in mind, we can now listen to and explore the long-term place of the adoption in the lives of the birth fathers in this study.

The Child in Mind

The research among birth mothers points to, for some, enduring feelings of motherhood in the years that follow adoption (Baran *et al.* 1977; Howe *et al.* 1992; Hughes and Logan 1993). Was there any parallel for these birth fathers? Did the child continue to 'exist' in their thoughts? If so how? And what of any other lasting thoughts and emotions, e.g. in connection with the birth mother? Many of the men had had regular and unexpected thoughts of the child throughout their lives after the adoption. A sense of a visitation came through in some accounts – one man likened the recurrence of thoughts of the child to the appearance of a ghost. Throughout their lives, feelings towards, and concerning, the child were present. These feelings, typically of a disturbing and moving nature, played a part in influencing the men's behaviour: precipitating marital discord, being more protective towards subsequent children. So when, why and how does the child 'persist'?

The men were asked to look over their lives from the adoption to present day, trying to exclude any recent motivation to search or contact. They were invited to comment on the appearance and recurrence or continuation of any feelings that may have related to the child. They were also asked to identify any triggers for such feelings. Twenty-eight men in the group were able to report in this area. The remaining two were unable to because they had become aware of the adoption many years after and so could not substantively discuss the child in their lives following the adoption. The responses are divided into two main groups: those men for whom post-adoption feelings subsided (this group includes the three men who had said that they felt very little after the adoption); and those for whom such feelings either did not ebb or increased in intensity. A discussion of each gives a flavour of the various degrees of presence of the child in the lives of the men.

Those Whose Feelings Subsided after the Adoption (14)

Half of those who could report on changes in their post-adoption feelings experienced an eventual reduction in feelings of distress. These men said that various feelings of loss, anger and powerlessness subsided in the weeks and months after the adoption: 'a void sort of closed up'. Notwithstanding this, they talked of the regular presence of the child in their thoughts in the following years. Accounts of the child's continuing 'existence' are diverse but typically one man put it that his child was 'always in mind. I have a kid out there. I always remembered his birthday'. Another man said that he had:

> ... never stopped loving him or caring for him. It's like I have a son somewhere out there and it can bring a smile to my face and other times it's like a glow. I just feel good. At other times I feel sad when I think about him.

One man was once struck by feelings that something untoward had happened to his son: 'I had this weird apprehension that something had happened to him during childhood. And I had to let him go, I had to pretend that he was dead.' This mechanism was apparently necessary because, to all intents and purposes, his son's welfare was beyond his control. One man's feelings subsided to a much greater extent than that of the others. Recurring thoughts of his daughter were less arresting although he sometimes wondered 'how she had turned out'.

There were many triggers for these thoughts. They arose for some when receiving professional help. More typically, birthdays were significant ('There's never a 7 March goes by without thoughts of him.') as was Christmas ('a bad time')'. Other triggers such as the sight of, and contact with, children who would be the same age as the child who was adopted were also mentioned. Also, there were thoughts of the child just 'at quiet moments'.

Those for Whom Feelings Persisted, Intensified or Emerged (14)

One man in this group said: 'It just never gets any better, the bitterness is still there'. Another's feelings also never changed and he added:

> It was terribly difficult to cope with. In the intervening years you wonder what she's like. It's her birthday. She's three. How was she getting on. Even to the fact that you wonder 'Is she still alive?'. Something could have happened to her. Not everybody survives childhood. 'Was the adoption successful?' Things triggered it. Suddenly seeing a little girl of that age.

Another man kept an account of his child's development via her birthdays:

> As time went by when I'd see a child, I'd think Beatrice must be that age. This feeling has become more pronounced as I've got older. There has never been a time when I was completely free.

In the case of another, there was a similar regularity with regard to the child's presence in his life: 'every day' with a 'wanting to know' his daughter.

The intensity of their feelings grew for some. The pregnancy and birth events had had little impact upon one man, however, during the adoption arrangements, he became progressively more agitated as to the welfare of his child. He opposed the adoption unsuccessfully and was then left with considerable feelings of regret that remained permanently close to the surface. His 'stack of emotional baggage' had always meant that he had been unable to think of her 'without feeling tearful and emotional'. This had intensified at certain times such as the births of subsequent children. Another man, five years after the adoption, undertook a search of all the primary schools in the area where his daughter would have likely to have been living – a feature of Parkes' conventional grief reaction as discussed earlier. Another explained that he married soon after the adoption. The subject of children inevitably arose and he began looking in prams for the son that had been adopted. One man said that the subject arose during counselling: 'It was actually on the day of his birthday. I had never seen it (the adoption) as my loss. Always only Yvonne's (the birth mother). I completely broke down and cried'.

It will be remembered that there were a few men who initially felt little or nothing after the adoption. For two of them thoughts and feelings in relation to the child emerged for the first time some years after. One had not felt anything because the adoption experience had made him emotionally 'blocked'. A second man's feelings concerning the adoption 'weren't a major problem' but three years after the event 'it started to grate on my mind. It was just there in your brain. The not knowing. Whether she's alive, whether she's alright.' The thoughts of the child are therefore diverse, impactful, frequent and capable of being triggered by a variety of experiences. But exactly who or what did these birth fathers think of? And how?

Thoughts of the Child

One of the many values of the only other study of birth father experiences and feelings is the range of feelings identified (Cicchini 1993). Feelings of 'sadness' are to the fore as are frustration, responsibility, guilt and helplessness. Also featured prominently are anger, emptiness, remorse, confusion, inadequacy and worry. Grief was reported by some. This range of feelings is associated with how the men thought of themselves as birth fathers, i.e. somewhat distinct from feelings about the child. Cicchini's study included feelings about the child (responsibility) alongside the men's feelings of being a birth father (helplessness and inadequacy). In this discussion feelings about the child are prioritised and I have separated feelings directly concerned with the child from those feelings that were more to do with the adoption, e.g. powerlessness.

Table 7.1 What do you feel when you think of the child?	
Curiosity	14
Parenthood	10
Worry/concern	9
Responsibility	7
Loss	6
Love	4
Guilt	4
Regret	3
Connected	2

The men's reports of how they think of the child were categorised on the basis of both explicit content and implicit meanings. For instance those who referred directly to 'a curiosity' were grouped in the category of that name; men who talked of 'wondering' about the child were included in the same group. The men who had had experience of contact (at the interview this varied from just one meeting to six years of being in touch) were asked to think back to how they had thought of the child before contact. The reports from this group of ten men therefore had a retrospective character that was influenced by the predominantly positive nature of the contact. However both groups, those with and without contact, gave remarkably similar accounts of how they thought (or had thought for those ten who now have contact) of their child. Most of them expressed more than one set of feelings but usually there was a primary one that dominated the response. The frequency of these is presented in Table 7.1, above.

Curiosity

Nearly half the group (14) referred to curiosity. Typical statements included: 'I'd just like to know what had happened to him, where he'd been, what he'd done. Just like to know, just like to know. Curiosity, simple curiosity'. And: 'When she was a teenager – "Is she going out dancing?, Is she married?, And has children?, How old is she now?"' The latter comment was made by a man who was unsure as to the month of his daughter's birth. Such curiosity is found too in accounts by birth mothers of how they think of their child, typically: 'All I really want to know is what happened to my son, how life has treated him, if he has been happy' (Powell and Warren 1997, p.75).

Concern or Worry

Curiosity shades from a mild emotion into a more concentrated type of interest that was concern or worry for nine men:

> I wonder what sort of person she is and, as I say, one then starts to worry about if there are tremendous difficulties in her life either caused by the adoption or just because of who she is. I suspect, although I don't know, because I don't have any other children, I suspect it is a parental worry that I have or it is a worry about, I suppose children in general – in a world full of drugs and muggings etc. It's a concern but it is also an interest.

One man became agitated: 'Is she alive, is she doing well?' ('If she wasn't and you knew where she was?' GC) 'Well I would steam in and help her. If she was a drug addict, or anything, if she was desperate, you'd help her'. This man's worry was also mixed with frustration over not being able to 'rescue' his daughter; the wish to do something was common to many. Anxiety about the child is also a feature in birth mother studies (Hughes and Logan 1993).

As curiosity shades into worry, so too does worry or concern overlap with feelings of responsibility: 'I worry about how abandoned she feels. Is she alive even? We want her to know if ever she needed us, we'd be there for her'.

Responsibility

Cicchini suggests that the sense of responsibility he found amongst birth fathers stems from a maturational process. Over the period from their teenage years to the time of the interview, the birth fathers in his study developed a sense of responsibility towards the child, part of becoming a mature adult (1993). Without an accurate account of the degree of responsibility felt at the time of the adoption, then a comparison with later years is difficult to make. What was concentrated upon here was the nature of birth father feelings at the time of the interview: in later life.

Seven of the birth fathers (almost a quarter of the group) described feelings of responsibility. Responsibility, obligation and duty were all words that were used to describe how they felt about the welfare of the child. Two men spoke of a feeling of 'duty' towards the child. One man spoke of his 'duty of care' in relation to the child, in his case to provide a father to her although he also felt he had not fulfilled his 'charge'. Another also spoke of duty:

> It's built up. I think brought on by my eldest daughter going to college – rites of passage – made me sort of start thinking. It was always there. I wouldn't say that I am doing it out of duty (registering on a contact register), but there is also a certain sense of duty. I'd love to know how she is, how she got on. I'd be frightened about it as well. But I very much want to be available for her.

Another man said that when he thought of his child: 'I still have all the parental feelings. They won't go away. It's a burden you can never put down.' Here there is a sense of having 'shouldered' a (painful) obligation at the point of having the child adopted.

The widespread belief that good fathers are those who provide (Lupton and Barclay 1997; Warin *et al.* 1999) is summed up in the birth father literature by a man who asks: 'Who am I if I am not a protector and a providing father?'(Rosenberg 1992, p.35). Such a belief and the feeling of having defaulted on this, would contribute to the men's enduring thoughts of worry and responsibility and could also be linked with feelings of guilt.

Parenthood

Overlapping with feelings of responsibility, duty or obligation, were feelings of parenthood. The majority of the studies of birth mothers have found a continuing sense of parenthood (Howe *et al.* 1992; Hughes and Logan 1993). Ten men in this study echo similar feelings:

> There's one missing in my family. I wonder what she's like. I think – waste of potential. I feel I have abandoned my charge. I regard her as my child. As one that's missing amongst my children.

and:

> I've got a fourteen year old in my mind's eye. At the end of the day, in one sense, you can only turn around and say 'She'll always be my little girl'. But I know she's fourteen, she'll be fifteen in June. She's no longer the madam who's growing up. She'll have her own ways.

This man also expressed a belief that he could not 'turn round and say "She's mine" because I've never met the girl. Although technically, in one sense, she is mine. On the other hand she isn't mine'. A division between social parent and biological father was made by four of these ten men:

> I wonder if she's ok, if she's healthy, if her parents are good to her. It depends who I'm speaking to but I sometimes say 'I've got three'. I think of Jennifer as a second daughter.

And: 'Although Susan, even if she came back, I'll never be her father. I'm her father biologically'. Here is the dilemma for many of the men: that of being the biological father and feeling like the father of a missing child – but without an outlet for the paternal feelings associated with that child.

Love

Two men talked of parenthood and explicitly linked this to love for their child. Another two talked about this love without directly referring to any feelings of parenthood:

> There is a sense in which, I don't know, whatever he's done or hasn't done; or what would happen if he'd turned out and been a murderer or rapist or you know, I would not love him any the less. I don't think I've ever stopped loving him. Or the thought of him.

It is probable that if most of the men were asked directly, they would indicate their feelings for the child in terms of love; however these four unsolicited statements of love were prompted by asking how they thought of their child. The men's accounts of love for their child were intermingled with feelings of an attachment or connection.

Connectedness

Two men said they felt a connectedness with their child: 'Who is he? What's his personality like? I wonder about someone out there that I'm close to. I feel like I know him'. And:

> It must be partly love. I'd love to see him. What I did was a wrong thing in one way. I thought we were making the right

decisions whatever. It goes against the grain. You're giving up somebody you instinctually love, is part of you.

This sense of a continuing connection and intimacy with the child is present in the birth mother research (Millen and Roll 1985; Weinreb and Murphy 1988). The (broken) connection was conveyed in their belief that part of them had been lost.

Loss

The literature suggests that the nature of the loss felt by birth mothers is that of the loss of the child (Inglis 1984; Sorosky *et al.* 1978; Winkler and van Keppel 1984).[1] In this study, whilst nearly all the men who spoke included feelings of loss in their accounts, six men spoke straight away to their feelings of loss when they thought of their child:

> I hope she's well, OK. Then a little bit of anxiety steps in. Help-lessness, you want to reach out to something you don't know where it is. You want to reach out and probably say who you are. (Why? GC) I still feel that she's a part of me. It's like something from inside of me is missing. Part of my being, in a way.

Loss was deeply felt by at least two of this group who spoke in physical terms:

> It's like, I don't know, it's like a finger cut off, thirty years ago. There's so much to be regretted because we lost this child for that length of time. That's an accurate assessment of the factors. That's what I feel.

---

1   What appears to be unexplored is whether this loss concerns anything other than the 'lost' child. Brodzinsky questions the use of the term 'sense of loss' in the research and argues that it is 'somewhat questionable as a construct when not theoretically grounded or operationally defined' (1990, p.303).

> There is not a day that goes by that I don't think of him. I feel as if there is something inside me that has been ripped out and I feel empty and nothing is going to fill that.

Feelings of physical loss are reported in the research on birth mothers (Roll *et al.* 1986; Sorosky *et al.* 1978). However, there was something else present in the men's accounts – the loss of missed opportunities to parent the child: 'I feel that I've been robbed of his childhood. Seeing him grow up and all his teething, taking him to parks and all that sort of thing, football games'. Here feelings were concerned with having lost out on shared activities with their child. Perhaps because fathering is defined by what a man *does*, birth fathers might tend to highlight feelings of missed activity with the child. There were connections between expressions of loss and feelings of regret. These also shade into each other.

Regret

Four men said that they had feelings of regret about the adoption when they thought of their child. In the case of one this included loss:

> I think of her as somebody I miss. Somebody that I've missed all these years. Miss the contact. Missed even seeing her as baby and I think that was totally unfair. I don't feel that I'm her natural father. Had I been present it wouldn't have happened. She would have a different sort of life.

In their accounts regret was a regular feature as the men looked back 30 years or more. The content of this feeling was diverse and sometimes difficult to uncouple from their feelings about their actions (or lack of them) and those for the child. There was regret that that they had not been more capable of preventing the adoption, either because they were not informed of the decision (as in the quote above), or because they were powerless to stop the proceedings as they unfolded. There was also regret and sadness at being absent at various milestones in their child's life, e.g. graduation.

Guilt

Four men felt guilt, typically: 'I feel guilty about the rich family life she could have had. I feel like we abandoned her'. The men associated these feelings of guilt with having not 'stood up' for themselves (and for the birth mother and the child), with not having done enough to prevent the adoption and, for those who agreed with the adoption (with hindsight perhaps) a belief that they had done something wrong. Responsibility for a wrong has been found in accounts of birth mother feelings in later life. Some have described themselves as 'rotten to the core' and 'needing to be punished' (Hughes and Logan 1993).

When the ten men who felt like fathers are added to the seven with a sense of responsibility, those who felt loss (2) and the two men who felt love and a 'connectedness', it can be seen that 21 men explicitly talked of the continued existence of the child in their inner lives in the years after the adoption. These are men who could be said to have (like birth mothers) 'retained a very clear understanding of their sons and daughters as people with whom they still felt the deepest bond' (Bouchier *et al.* 1991, p.108).

A subsidiary question is also raised concerning the possibility of the gendered nature of such feelings of connectedness. Are there differences between birth fathers' thoughts of boys and their thoughts of girls? Do their thoughts of boys include a regret for traditional father/son activities such as football? Do their thoughts of girls include notions that they may be in need of protection? This may be an interesting subject for research with a larger study group and is also an area that has not been explored in the birth mother literature.

The term 'connectedness' seems fitting for the above group of child-centred, emotionally charged thoughts. The fact that such a connectedness exists in the case of men who have never parented the child in question is surprising, even more so given that in some cases the child had never been seen. This is a finding that suggests a rethink of conventional notions of fatherhood; in particular those ideas that suggest men derive their feelings of parenthood from a process of active participation in social caring for the child. This connectedness, and its resonances with the experiences of birth mothers, is a central discovery and has many implications for policy and practice – not least the need to now include birth fathers in the adoption 'triangle'.

Relationships with the Birth Mother Before and After the Adoption and Later Life Thoughts of her

The birth mother has been a key but silent figure so far. Very early in the interviews it became clear that the men were talking of past *and* present thoughts and feelings about the birth mother. As we shall see, even if relationships failed there were meetings with her following the adoption and sometimes contact, mostly considerably later in life. The pictures that emerge provide an additional insight into the inner lives of some of these birth fathers. Studies of birth mother experiences (when they refer to the birth father at all) have generally been confined to reporting the facts of the relationship between birth parents at the time of the adoption, for example stating whether or not it was a steady relationship (Hughes and Logan 1993). Where it has been discussed, it has been found that many birth mother and birth father relationships were steady and not casual (Triseliotis 1970; Wells 1993b).

Overall, there has been little previous exploration of the quality, nature and outcome of the relationship between birth mother and birth father. Indeed a key piece of research set out to interview women who were 'neither married, had been married, nor in a stable de facto relationship at the time of relinquishment' (Winkler and van Keppel 1984, p.29). Additionally it appears that birth mothers' later-life thoughts of the birth father have not been explored. Yet often during contact between birth mothers and their (adult) children the issue of the birth father (whether forgotten or not) arises for the birth mothers. This is because he may become the subject of the adopted child's curiosity and search after they have found their birth mother (March 1995, p.110–117). For a considerable proportion of the men, either the birth mother lived on in their feelings, or he and she continued to have a relationship. What part did the adoption experience have in these birth father–birth mother relationships? This section also discusses the men's later-life thoughts concerning the birth mother.

Twenty-one Relationships that Ceased

In nine cases relationships drifted, ended or had somehow been damaged. One man said that he and the birth mother had agreed to part after the adoption: '...we both wanted to share the emotion. And couldn't. Sad'. For four men, the birth mother ended it. One man said that she had felt unable to continue their relationship: 'She felt guilty, devastation. We both felt mutual distress. She said to stop because of the pain'. This man telephoned the birth mother a number of times to talk about the child but she found the calls too upsetting and asked him to cease. One birth mother ended the relationship before the child was born because she believe that their child had been the result of his rape of her. Another birth mother ended the relationship immediately after the birth of the child. Parents or external authorities such as social workers compulsorily ended the relationship in at least four cases. Three of the men were responsible for the end of the relationship. One fled on the news of pregnancy, another declined an offer to continue after the adoption and the third man left the country some months after the adoption.

It is difficult to generalise from the reasons given for the end of these 21 steady relationships. The motives appear to be varied, and of course, truth is relative. However it appears that for most, whether the relationship ended during the pregnancy or after the adoption, what had been stable relationships ended as a result of the overall experience. The two key causes appear to be that, first, the relationship could not continue in the light of the discomfort and distress generated during the adoption process, and second, forces other than the birth father or the birth mother ended the relationship. The end of these steady relationships was seen by many of the men as a matter of regret.

Seven Relationships that Continued

There were seven men who continued in long-term relationships with the birth mother. Two were married; three became married; and two carried on the relationship. At the time of the interview two of these relationships were intact. All of the men talked of relationship difficulties arising from either an inability to discuss the adoption experience or their personal distress. One man and the birth mother married because:

> After the adoption we both felt that we had a duty to one another and we both felt that it was the right thing to do – not the basis for a marriage. I felt that we got married and stuck together; the reward was that she would one day get in touch with us.

He said that on reflection (during the interview) this mutual expectancy must have been their way of dealing with the negative emotional aftermath of the adoption. However, he and she never spoke about it. This is also a characteristic of the other relationships. Three out of the five marriages ended; two divorces were said to have happened because of the distress arising from unresolved and unspoken feelings about the adoption. In the case of one man who did not marry yet continued his relationship with the birth mother, the relationship ended because he wanted to have a (second) child but felt he could not. To have had another child with the birth mother would have been 'too painful to bear' as it would have brought back distressing memories of the adoption of their first child.

We split up about two years later. I'm putting it down to the strain of it. I thought that subconsciously if I left, then the past would go with it. Her having the baby stopped us from being normal teenagers.

The Adverse Effects of the Adoption on all Birth Mother–Birth Father Relationships

Birth parents in both groups – those in relationships that ceased at the time and those in relationships that continued – appear to have been adversely affected by the adoption experience. The events of the pregnancy, birth and adoption generated considerable emotional turbulence and distress and it seems that the end of the birth father–birth mother relationship was a consequence of this. Notwithstanding this, the birth fathers in this study report that they played a significant part in the events and that the relationship with the birth mother was important to both of them. Yet the research to date has cast the birth mother as the sole party involved. Studies that make no further reference to the birth father may then convey the impression that his emotional (and physical) involvement in the events was minimal. For example, Hughes and Logan (1993) report that in 16 out of 27 cases the birth mother was either abandoned by the birth father or that they lost contact. No differentiation is made between desertion and the relationship ending, perhaps (as indicated in this study) because of external pressures or the negative emotional effects of the adoption.

By omitting to explore the nature of the birth mother–birth father relationship, previous birth mother studies have therefore provided only a one-dimensional and erroneous impression of the birth father. However a more rounded and informed picture of the birth *parent* experience and birth parent relations with each other has emerged in this study. Here there is evidence of a more mutually but differently experienced series of events in which the birth father has played a not insignificant part. In short, from this study, the adoption happened to both the birth mother and the birth father.

Later-life Contact with the Birth Mother

For some men a wish to re-establish a relationship with the birth mother was a powerful feeling that affected their relationships with subsequent partners. In some cases this was not acted upon, however, a few men did renew their contact with the birth mother.

Many of the men whose relationship with the birth mother either ended during the pregnancy or shortly after, reported subsequent contact with her. Of the 21 men who parted with the birth mother, 16 had contact with her after the adoption. This subsequent contact was an unexpected but recurring feature in the lives of many of the men. It seems that none of the birth mother studies have explored whether or not there had been any contact following the adoption or the nature of this. For some of the men, continued knowledge of and possible contact with the birth mother would not have been unexpected, given that they both lived in the same community or neighbourhood or that there were shared aspects of their lives. For instance, they were both at college or moved in the same circles or 'crowd' – in one case they were both members of the same theatre company. Therefore contact (as distinct from a relationship) either continued or reoccurred. And, as we shall see, irrespective of whether they were ever in touch again, some men talked of powerful thoughts and feelings held for the birth mother.

Meetings with the birth mother ranged from unexpected encounters on the bus or in the street in the months after the adoption, to having met again as a result of their (now adult) child having traced one or both of them. A considerable number of the men talked of meetings, by chance or by arrangement, telephone or letter contact and in at least two cases the re-commencement of a relationship. In one case the two had met three months after the adoption. She wanted to resume the relationship. He did not. He gave as his reason that he had been 'disgusted' by her post-natal body shape. In some of the meetings, even those that were unexpected, heated exchanges about the child, the adoption and their relationship took place.

One man reported a regular annual phone conversation on or near the anniversary of their son's birth as well as having had two or three meetings with the birth mother, years apart and in different parts of the UK. Another four men reported efforts to meet and talk about the adoption – in three of these cases, many years after. Two men had aspirations and made efforts to 'begin again' – to re-establish a relationship with the birth mother. These men made considerable efforts to contact birth mothers who were by then married and living in, respectively, Canada and Australia. Whether or not subsequent contact had taken place, nearly a quarter of the group (7/30) held strong positive feelings for the birth mother. These dated from a time of between 25 and 30 years since the adoption. One man was:

> ...still carrying a torch for her. And that there was a sense in which throughout our whole marriage of 25 years, I have to say, I think that the ghost of Christine (the birth mother) existed.

Their feelings for the birth mother were influential: 'One of the difficulties that I've had probably, is that other people, especially women in my life, have probably emotionally had to be scored against Carol. That's not easy for somebody else to live up to'. Another man leant over to me and said in a whisper (so that his wife who was nearby at the time could not hear) that he '...still loved her. That never changed. I've been married for thirty years and although I would never say it in front of my wife, I still love her. Never been the same without her'. Two men said that on learning that the birth mother was to be married, they had secretly attended the marriage ceremony.

The depth of these feelings was striking; typically: 'She was *the* girl'. At the time of the interview, two men had begun affairs with the birth mother; in one case they had both been married to others and in the second case, she was married but not he. Not only was there a sense of a first love lost but also the men seemed to regret this loss. In view of the men's ages at the time – for most of them the birth mother had been their first sexual partner – and the unexpected circumstances that brought their relationship to an end, it is not surprising that feelings of loss of a (possible life) partner and wistfulness hung in the air.

Not all of them spoke so fondly. One man held no positive feelings of what might have been. On the contrary, he was forthright in expressing a low opinion of the birth mother and their relationship ended whilst he was in prison. He reported that she had been the prime mover in this and had not come to visit him:

> I think it was probably just a case that I was a young boy of 18 and she was 24 years old – she was pregnant and I loved her. She asked me to marry her one day and I said yes. It's really hard to explain. Basically if I had never met her none of this would have happened. But then again I wouldn't have had my son.

One other man said that his negative feelings for the birth mother had directly inhibited him from developing close relationships with other women and men. A third expressed bitterness because of the way that he had been 'manipulated and used' to provide the birth mother with a child. Most of the men did not meet up again with the birth mother, but the end of their relationship did not prevent feelings for her playing a significant part in the men's lives. Such feelings, whether regret, nostalgia or sentimentality, may have contributed to their sense of loss. In an extreme case one man's account was devoted more to his feelings for the birth mother than any other single factor in the adoption experience. He spent less time discussing the child than he did relating the history of his involvement with the birth mother and his attempts to locate her after the adoption. There is evidence elsewhere of birth fathers' continuing feelings towards the birth mother (Concerned United Birthparents 1983). Perhaps on this point birth fathers do differ from birth mothers – certainly the inner worlds of the men in this study have included the birth mother many years after the adoption.

The Effect of the Adoption on Subsequent Relations with Other Partners

Eighteen out of a total of 30 men had experienced separations or divorces. This seemingly high rate of relationship breakdown was attributed to the detrimental effect of the adoption experience. Four of the separations or divorces involved a second or third long-term relationship. At the time of the interview some of the men were in the midst of separating from a long-term partner. Two men were leaving their wives and children. One man was in the middle of being left as I arrived for the interview. Two other men talked of current disharmony in their marriages. Another man was in the midst of his second divorce. Seven out of the 30 drew connections between feelings about the adoption and the child and their experiences of marital or relationship discord. One man's wife had left him for someone else because he had been too 'withdrawn'. Another said that his failure to commit to a partner was because of caution derived from his negative experiences of the adoption. A third man's feelings for the child had been a 'source of tension' in his marriage. Another said that his feelings about the child were a 'secret set of emotions' in his two marriages. One man blamed his divorce (from the birth mother) on the negative adoption experience. Another said that his marriage breakdown and subsequent divorce from the birth mother were also the consequence of negative feelings about the adoption, carried by both of them.

Five men indicated that soon after the adoption they had married 'on the rebound'. These marriages were not necessarily disharmonious, though some turned out to be so. Four said that their inability to talk about their feelings for their child had caused strain in their marriages or long-term relationships. Either they felt that they were unable to share them; or such feelings were received with lack of sympathy:

> I don't think I had come to terms with all these feelings. In a way I hoped that marriage would help that, but it didn't. I felt that when I wanted to open up about Daniel and my feelings about that, I often got it chucked back in my face. He was a presence in our marriage and during many arguments.

Another man remarked that the adoption had had a negative impact upon his partner and this had 'sexually affected' their relationship – 'destroyed it'. At the time of the interview three of these marriages or long-term relationships had ended.

A fourth man's experience provides a counterpoint to the suggestion that marriages or relationships ended because of unsympathetic partners. In this case, his partner, on hearing of the adoption, circled the adopted child's birth date on the New Year's calendar. She did this every year. This was clearly received as a supportive action yet at the time of the interview their marriage was breaking up. Here the discord could not be attributed to his partner's lack of sympathy. In another three cases, partners were supportive and had enabled the men to talk about their feelings regarding the adopted child. In other cases, however, either their feelings were not insistent enough to have been a matter for mutual exploration, or thoughts regarding the child had lain dormant and were not shared with partners.

Two other men said that a combination of distressful feelings about the adoption and their feelings regarding the child contributed to the break-up of relationships. Neither man was able to separate out their feelings of distress from thoughts of the child. In both cases the issue had surfaced whilst they were in contact with counsellors for reasons ostensibly unconnected with the adoption. Both sets of emotions co-existed for these two men. For one there was a definite 'pining for my baby' accompanied by feelings of helplessness and anxiety related to his inability to have prevented the adoption. The second man retained feelings of powerlessness and isolation engendered by the adoption process. He also had feelings of 'loss and grief' directly related to the child. Both men reported initial feelings of being 'blocked' when asked how they had felt at the time of the adoption, but both experienced the sudden emergence of these feelings some years after.

Others believed that the adoption experience had influenced their general attitude to all relationships. One man had been made 'bitter'; another was 'unlucky in love'. Two others – in terms of the adoption's effect – had been made 'cynical' and 'hardened' in their attitudes towards relationships. Another man 'wasn't a very pleasant person to women in that period. I was very bitter'. These men believed that their negative attitudes originated in the experience of loss and disenfranchisement during the adoption.

Thus, a diversity of thoughts and feelings influenced the men's subsequent adult relationships. These range from feelings for the birth mother, feelings of anger and distress arising from the upset of the adoption, to thoughts of the child which inhibited the development of relationships. This group of disparate thoughts and feelings (all arising from the one emotionally salient period) is complex. There is no single determining element inhibiting the men's relationships. In terms of directly attributable effects of the adoption (there may be other unrelated factors), there were feelings of nostalgia concerning a possible family life with the birth mother and adopted child and an enduring love (or at the least a strong affection) for the birth mother. Additionally, negative emotions provoked by their experiences of the adoption and persistent thoughts of the child were also influences that flawed their relationships with others. Parallels with these findings (regarding the adoption's detrimental effect on subsequent relationships) are found in birth mothers' accounts (Deykin *et al.* 1984; Rosenberg 1992). These points may be of interest, where a man is a birth father, and taken into the reckoning of those who work with men and their relationships, e.g. in the field of marriage guidance and couple counselling.

If then there is evidence of the adoption's impact upon adult relationships, how was the experience of becoming a parent (for most men, for the second time) affected?

Parenting

Most men (21/30) went on to parent other children; six talked of feeling over-protective. One man said that 'I treated June (his next child after the one that was adopted) special because she was the first baby daughter I had hands on with'. For others the birth of their next child brought forth feelings and memories from the previous experience. At the births of their other children two men thought 'I've done this before but gave it away' and 'I'll never replace the one that got away'. Before the birth another hoped that he would have a girl – to replace the one who had been adopted. More positive views were also expressed: a determination to be present at the birth in the light of having been banned from the birth of the child that had been adopted.

One man drew a comparison between the son that was adopted and a second son. His relationship with his second son was not as close as he would have hoped. He also wondered whether he and the adopted son would have been closer:

> I suppose the bit that I feel about Michael is that a bit of me feels, well, I would love to have somebody who's, you know, possibly just that bit closer, somebody who would take me out for a pint.

Another man felt similar feelings of disappointment in relation to his (second) son's lack of interest in athletics – he too speculated as to whether the adopted son would have turned out more 'sporty'. In the accounts of the latter two men there may be a certain idealisation of 'the one that got away'.

One man, when asked about his feelings after the birth and adoption, explained these both in terms of having a substitute and of gender divisions:

> I suppose I blanked it. Yeh, I suppose I was disappointed. I never saw her (the child), there was no hands on. Psychologically it was a different kettle of fish from a man and a woman. We're not the same as women, are we? I was disappointed. I wasn't hurt. I had Natalie (step-daughter), another daughter.

For him his step-parenting role took the place of any activity that would have happened with his first (adopted) daughter; thus alleviating any negative feelings that may have endured as a result of the adoption. His views and feelings provide a counterpoint to any suggestion that all birth fathers may feel a sense of loss as regards their adopted child. This man seemed to have had his need to parent a daughter satisfied with a substitute, although he is amongst those men who began to determinedly search for their children, suggesting that this was not sufficient.

Many of the men described a dilemma that crops up for birth mothers (Howe *et al.* 1992, p.77): how to respond when the subject of number of children arises? For instance, on official forms and, if they had not had another child of the same sex as the adopted one, when asked whether they regretted not having a boy/girl. Most of the men included the adopted child. Typically he/she was 'not a secret'; others were open with partners and those whom they felt that they could confide in: 'In the family I always used to say that I had three daughters'. Other men did not include the child that was adopted but would mentally anguish about this 'difficult area':

> When I go for jobs and you get application forms and they ask if you have any children. Inside I know I have to put 'no'. I feel like I am denying my son because he is not in my house and therefore I have not got a son. When in company and you say I have got a son but he is not around then they start wondering why.

Other men alternated between doing so and not, depending on the circumstances: 'I think of myself as a father of four children but I say this when I feel safe'.

A significant number of men (9/30) had had no other children. For five men of this group (5/9) the adopted child was their only child. One man felt that the responsibility of having other children was so great that he had delayed so long that the time had past. He had had a vasectomy. Two others said that they had never felt that they had had the kind of relationships that encompassed the possibility of a (second) child of their own. Four of the nine who did not father a child again had had children prior to the one that was adopted. One of these men said that the adoption experience had put him off having more children. A second said that after the adoption he had 'never wanted another'. These two men had been opposed to the adoption (and were married to the birth mother at the time). A third man said that had he known of the adoption plans at the time he would have opposed them. The fourth had been in favour of the adoption.

Irrespective of the men's parenting 'career' either before or after the adoption, nearly all of their attitudes to parenting again were influenced by the adoption experience and their thoughts and feelings about the child that had been adopted. It has been shown that this is also the case in relation to their behaviour and attitudes with subsequent children. It should also be noted that as featured earlier, some birth father relationships with their own parents were detrimentally affected by the adoption.

Emergent Themes in Life after the Adoption

Two significant elements emerge in the narratives of the birth fathers in this study. The first is the child's continuing 'existence' in their thoughts. This presence in their minds and daily lives is felt as a connection to the child. Second, the birth mother and her place in the men's subsequent lives; the influence of feelings for her and, as I have pointed out, her continued presence in the inner (and sometimes actual) lives of the men.

Various life events were referred to and assessed: successful and unsuccessful marriages, births of subsequent children and bereavements, their physical and mental health. There were other diverse, impactful events, e.g. one man said that his gay son's 'coming out' was an event of extreme importance to him. One man described his marriage as life enhancing, in direct contrast to the effect of the adoption. One man identified his first foreign holiday as an important milestone in his life. Another recalled getting arrested during a 'mods and rockers' seaside confrontation as part of his life's significant events.

In their responses to how they might rate the position of the adoption amongst their life events, either before or after the adoption, two men said that the adoption was less significant than the death of their fathers. Another two men said that the impact of a divorce and the birth of a child subsequent to the one that was adopted superceded the effect and influence of the adoption in their lives. For three men the adoption's impact was 'about the same' as other significant experiences and events. Of this group, one man had had a long life (he was 79 at the time of the interview) and had experienced a number of bereavements such as the death of a second wife and the early deaths of a son and daughter. The second said about the adoption that: 'The only thing that I would say was as much hurt was when my dad died. That hurt'. The third equated the emotional impact of the adoption as the same as his distress when his wife had left him.

The reports of the other 23 birth fathers suggested that the emotional impact of the adoption was more deep and lasting than almost anything else that had happened to them: 'One of the major happenings in my life'. For many the adoption and loss of their child was a milestone or 'peak' on a graph of the emotional and psychological geography of their lives:

> In terms of a life graph through to the birth of my next children, it would be very high. Highest thing around, because going off to college and A levels was no big deal. It was a different world in those days. It (the adoption) was a very big event and I wouldn't think that there was really anything much to compare with it.

There were differences of emphasis. There were those who spoke of the adoption and its effects as having had the greatest impact on their lives and those who felt that there had been other equally great events in their lives, yet rated the adoption as 'up there' with other positive and negative highlights. Three men specifically likened the effects of the adoption to that of a bereavement but observed: 'A death is just that. It's something that's gone', unlike the adoption where 'there is no end to the consequences'.

There are a number of similarities between the men's thoughts and feelings down through the years and those reported by birth mothers. The research on birth mothers has found evidence of 'a feeling that a bond continues between the birth mother and child even after adoption and continues throughout life' (Hughes and Logan 1993, p.90). The fact that the men in this study continue to think of the child, with some expressing a connectedness with it, indicates the existence of a more shared birth mother and birth father post-adoption experience than has hitherto been generally imagined. Other similarities can be seen in the men's relationships with partners and subsequent children. Where there appears to be less of a parallel is in relation to the men's thoughts of the birth mother.

A final point in this overview of the men's accounts of of life after the adoption is less central but just as intriging. This concerns some men's experiences of loss *prior* to the adoption.

Emergent Experiences of Bereavement or Major Loss Prior to the Adoption

Nine men spoke of a major loss or separation in their lives before the adoption. For five of them a parent had died (over a year before for all but one whose father died during the pregnancy). In the case of the other four men, one's mother had suffered a serious life-threatening illness (cerebral haemorrhage) and been hospitalised for a long time; a second man was separated from his parents when he was ten and sent from Brazil to boarding school in England and a third's parents divorced when he was four years old. The fourth man's life had been 'troubled' by the knowledge of his 'illegitimacy' – he did not know who his father was. In their accounts there was no link between previous experiences of loss and behaviour likely to result in a pregnancy and the adoption decision. However research among a larger sample of birth mothers (Raynor 1971) found that a similar proportion of women (16/56) had also experienced prior parental loss or separation. The figures were simply reported. Neither Bouchier *et al.* (1991) nor Mander (1995) explore similar evidence of birth mothers' prior experiences of bereavement or loss. Pannor *et al.* suggest an association between low self-esteem because of previous parent loss and unplanned pregnancies, with low self-esteem perhaps finding an outlet in sexual promiscuity and an unwillingness to use contraception (1971, p.120). Another point is that the men's second loss – the adoption of their child – may have been more distressing because of the earlier experience. On the other hand, they may have been better prepared for feelings of loss, depending upon how they had coped with the first loss, although from their accounts this does not seem to have been the case.

Overall almost all of the men in this study had thoughts of the child that was adopted and some of them held feelings of a bond with their child. For some there was a feeling of fatherhood, devoid of any social or physical focus. Thus the experiences and consequences of having been a birth father resonate in their subsequent lives. The adoption experience, feelings for their child and emotions concerning the birth mother form a constellation of thoughts and feelings that are long lasting and are seen by the men as formative and influential. The adoption of their child had come to be an important milestone in their life's journey.

The next chapter now goes on to explore what exactly it was that motivated the men to want contact with an (adult) son or daughter. And for those men who have met their child, the question is raised of how their feeling of a bond or 'connectedness' translates into reality.

Chapter Eight

Birth Father and Child: Towards Meeting and the Meanings of Contact

Is she alive? Well? Happy?

It would be useful if research could explore what practice and anecdotal accounts suggest – that some birth fathers at least do experience grief and a continuing need for reunion. (Mullender and Kearn 1997, p.20)

Although the majority of reports (21) did not include accounts of contact with the adopted child, hopes for such an event have or had become an important factor in the lives of most of the entire group of thirty men.[1] What was the overall position at the time of interview?

---

1 The figures for contact and non-contact are made up of 31 accounts. Twenty-one accounts from men who have not had experience of contact and ten from those who have. This is greater than the number of men in the study (30) because one man features twice: once for contact with one child and again in his account of seeking contact with a second, also adopted, child.

Awaiting Contact (16)

Altogether 16 men had placed their names and addresses on Adoption Contact Registers (ACRs) or with a social work or adoption agency. Nine of them felt that they had done as much as they could do: 'It is now up to her, if she wishes to find me she can'. They expressed a concern that the child's life should not be disrupted. If and when the child became curious enough to search, then details of where they could be contacted were now available. Five others expressed a view that they would take steps to initiate contact with the child if they knew how to.

At least three men had been active in attempting to contact the child. One man had previously and unsuccessfully engaged the services of a private detective. Actions like this and attempts to subvert the official ban as to the adopted person's identity are not uncommon (Coleman and Jenkins 1998, pp.39–46). In a letter to the newsletter of the Natural Parents Network (NPN), one birth mother spoke of 'loopholes in the system' (NPN No.18 1998). The NPN newsletter has now and then carried letters that offer suggestions to aid the search process. The ethics of this intense form of search activity have been considered mostly from only the birth parents' perspective. It is argued that such activity is forced on birth parents because of a lack of official sympathy from adoption agencies, a need to provide explanations for the adoption and a desire to ascertain the welfare of the adopted child (Coleman and Jenkins *op. cit.*).

The accounts of such search activity are imbued with a number of themes, including the justification that adopted people have the ability to trace their birth parents whereas the same does not apply to the other party. Also present is a sense of something akin to excitement – energy is generated in the decision to act perhaps after having remained in distress for a number of years: '…the process of doing it myself, I think, was very therapeutic. The fact that a birth mother has lost something and then tries to find it herself made more sense' (Coleman and Jenkins *op. cit.* p.46). McWhinnie has pointed out that the needs of the adopted person do not seem to feature in the birth parent literature (1994). Elsewhere the possibility of an unresponsive son or daughter has been noted: 'I thought she had a real nerve trying to come back into my life after all these years. She didn't want me in 1961, she sure as hell wasn't going to come back into my life now!' (adopted person quoted in Coleman and Jenkins *op. cit.* p.52). The majority of the group, whether having had contact or not, had not actively searched. One man had 'taken things as far as they could go' with the various agencies involved in the adoption.

The group of 16 that were awaiting contact expressed varying degrees of satisfaction. The amount of time between their decision to place their contact details on file, or on a register and the interview varied considerably. At least two men had done this as soon as they knew that the child was of an age to access his or her original birth certificate. In their eyes, this was the moment when the child could (and hopefully would) look for them. One man had, since the birth of his child, been in regular contact with the adoption agency regarding news of her welfare and to communicate any change of address. Others had utilised the services of the ACRs on hearing of their establishment. In the case of at least two men, they put their names down when these registers were launched in the early 1980s. One man had placed his name on an ACR a year before the interview. This was due to a combination of radio and television coverage and feelings engendered by the departure of his oldest (not the adopted) child for college. However the majority had made their names and addresses available many years ago.

Actively Seeking Contact (5)

Five men were actively seeking contact and had been doing so for two or three years prior to the interview. All of the men in this group had also placed their names and addresses with an agency that would forward these to the child if he or she so wanted. These men were also searching. Some were attempting to locate the child by combing through adoption and birth certificates that they had purchased in the hope that they could glean sufficient details to establish the new identity of the child. Others were using the mediation services of the original adoption agency or whatever agency now had possession of the adoption papers.

With Contact (10)

Four men had been traced by their (now adult) child. The other six men had either found their son or daughter or had been contacted because their names were on an ACR.

Table 8.1 How contact came about	
Actively traced by birth father	2
Traced by adopted person via mutual entries on ACR	4
Unexpectedly traced by adopted person	4

N = 10

At the time of the interview, contact with the adopted child (now adult) had been in place between four months and six years. The average length of time since contact was almost three years: 34 months. For all the men in the study, what are and were the reasons for wanting to meet their child?

The Motives for Contact – All

Aside from the group of four men who were unexpectedly contacted, the other 26 had each wished for or wish contact with the child. There is a retrospective quality in the responses of the ten men that had had contact with their child. Motives recalled after a positive meeting might have been different if such a meeting had been a bad experience. The men in question were asked to recall (as much as they could) what had been their thoughts prior to contact.

The motives for contact were various. A majority (15/26) expressed a curiosity as to 'how he (*sic*) turned out'; others felt a concern or worry. One man said he had an anxiety that being adopted may have led to his daughter feeling 'abandoned'. A large group of men (13/26) included in their motives the wish for an opportunity to make expiation as a means of relieving guilt caused by the adoption and their failure to have provided an alternative at the time. In the words of one man: 'To tell her that I am sorry for letting her be adopted'. There were others (8/26) who wanted to have 'some sort of relationship' that, in the eyes of some of them, might approximate to that of father and child. Included in the contact motives of three men were references to a need to complete their own personal and inner 'jigsaw'.

Curiosity and Concern

For half the men (15) the need for contact with their child was because of a growing curiosity or concern as to the child's well being. This feeling was previously found in how they thought of their child, before any decision to seek contact. The need for contact was seen by some men as the culmination of a process that had begun in the years following the adoption. This concern expressed itself in sentiments such as wanting to make themselves available to help, typically: 'Why do I want to meet her? To know if she is alive, happy? To see if she is alright', and 'I have a duty to her. I'd love to know how she is, how she's got on. To be available'. Rather than a process of a gradually increasing curiosity or, in some cases, concern, four other men said that the child's coming of age had been a decisive moment. This was significant because it was the time when they knew that the child could legally access his or her original certificate and thus know their birth father's name. One of these men anticipated a 'knock on the door'. There is much here that is echoed in the experiences of birth mothers (Bouchier *et al*. 1991).

Expiation

Where there are other parallels with the birth mother experience is in the presence of feelings of guilt (Winkler and van Keppel 1984). There were a number of references to the need to make some form of explanation or apology as to the circumstances of the adoption: 'To say I would have loved her, to apologise. To say I have carried on loving her', and: 'How is he doing? If I could help. Have some sort of relationship. It would be a relief for me. To explain my side. There is guilt in a way'. The need to apologise or 'put their side' was derived from their feelings of an inevitability or powerlessness relating to the adoption and a need to explain the circumstances at the time: 'To tell her I'm sorry'. In most cases, 'putting their side' consisted of explaining the circumstances in which both birth father and birth mother had found themselves; to say that 'it was not really our fault'. If one man was to meet his daughter he would, among other things, tell her that:

> I didn't want her to be adopted. Never ever did. She mustn't hold it against us because it was not really our fault. 'You weren't a casual affair to a couple who weren't going to get married. The powers that be said "No, you can't"'.

An exception to this sentiment was the case of one man whose wish to 'put the story right' was because the child was the result of his alleged rape of the birth mother. He felt that child would not receive an accurate (i.e. his) account of the circumstances of her conception.

The need to explain included a desire for absolution. Contact could be an opportunity to 'see if he'd blamed me'. Another man thought he might get 'a belt in the mouth' from his adopted daughter; he had felt to blame for the adoption and her anger would be justified. The men's need for expiation was combined with other more selfish motives:

> Some sort of relationship with him would be a relief for me. It's something I would like. I'm not going to force it because I think it has to come from the other side. But if it did come I would try

and establish a relationship. I suppose it's guilt in a way. Because one of the things I would want to do is to explain my side of the story. I know it is very selfish. But the decisions taken then were in David's best interest, at the time as we saw fit.

In light of the fact that some of this group concurred with the adoption decision at the time, it seems therefore that the guilty thoughts in question, and feelings of a need to apologise, are sentiments that have appeared at some time *after* the adoption. Cicchini suggests that this is the result of emotional maturation and a consequent growth in feelings of responsibility (1993).

A 'Restitution of the Self'

Three men spoke of their desire for contact as also motivated by a need to complete an 'unfinished jigsaw': 'Why contact? She's part of me, is she happy? To fill in a few empty spaces'. A similar analogy of 'missing pieces of a puzzle' features in the search and contact motivations of adopted people (Triseliotis 1973, p.81; March 1995, p.70). Does the 'jigsaw' metaphor convey something about how birth fathers are uniquely affected by adoption? Feelings of emptiness are found in studies of birth mothers' feelings in the years after the adoption (Howe *et al.* 1992, p.84) and it may be that here there are simply two different ways of expressing what is essentially the same loss. Indeed one man's motivations for contact closely resembled birth mothers' motivations: 'It's like something inside of me is missing'. Notwithstanding this man's reasons, it may be that, for those birth fathers who use the analogy of the unfinished jigsaw, they are expressing something slightly different: a need to make things 'right' by completing their life history, incomplete because of being excluded from the adoption process.

These men would not have knowledge of such facts as weight of the child, time of birth, descriptions of adoptive parents and the area of the country in which the child was to be brought up. In some cases the men never knew what the child had looked like. The relative knowledge that the birth mother gains of such matters is a product of her more central involvement in the adoption. Thus a gender difference in reasons for contact may be in evidence here that may arise from the circumstantially different experiences of each party at the time of the adoption. The birth fathers knew relatively less of the facts and this could explain their talk of something 'unfinished' and references to 'empty spaces' in some kind of stock-taking of their own inner world. This would mean that adoption workers may need to pay close attention to such details when working with birth fathers.

Where the men's reports and those of birth mothers show some parallels is in the notion that motives for search activity contain an element of self-interest. Deykin *et al.* comment that 'search activity may be a means of achieving restitution not of the surrendered child, but of the self' (1984, p.279). In other words, one of the motives for searching may be to be more at ease with oneself. Hughes suggests that, for birth mothers, one of the long-term effects of adoption is the possibility of mental ill health (1996). Those who choose to search may hope that contact will ameliorate their mental distress or the feeling of not being a mentally whole person. Such a feeling of a lack of wholeness or negative self-esteem (Weinreb and Cody Murphy 1988) may equate with the sense of being without restitution to which Deykin *et al.* refer. In the words of one birth father, he needed to begin searching 'to keep me sane'. Another man said that a relationship with his son would be 'a relief'. Berryman reports that one of the search motives for birth mothers is to obtain a 'sense of relief and peace of mind' (1997, p.311). Modell quotes a birth mother on finding her son: 'These are liminal moments, of being outside of self and simultaneously completing self – "feeling whole again"' (1986, p.655). Such self-help seems to be an additional element in the men's motivation to search.

Such motivations, however, form part of a complex group of thoughts and feelings that also include more altruistic reasons for seeking contact. Any dichotomy between personal need and altruism (as suggested by Deykin *et al.*) may not exist. In the search motives of the men it appears that meeting a personal need and an aspiration to 'do right' by the child are factors that co-exist. Malcolm's account (see below) seems to capture many of the elements of the men's motives for contact. He is concerned about his daughter's welfare, he has a personal sense of the loss of her in his life and he wants to tell her the facts behind her adoption. He also sees the recovery of his mental health as bound up with a successful search for his daughter.

Malcolm

Losses such as the death of his father and father-in-law (to whom he was very close) triggered feelings about his daughter, Karen, who was adopted whilst he was serving overseas. These feelings were buried until nine months prior to interview. He was going through a bad time: sleeping badly, unsettling dreams, crying a lot at work. He was on tranquilisers and thought he was going mad: 'totally to do with the adoption'. He realised then that he had to do something about Karen.

Malcolm researched the possibility of finding her and discovered that it might be possible if he were to buy the adoption certificates for a female child in the Court area where he remembered he'd been told her adoptive parents lived. By the time of the interview Malcolm had unsuccessfully spent nearly £1000 in the hope that he would discover a certificate that corresponded with Karen's birthday and even better one where her adoptive parents had either kept her first name or used it as a middle one.

Before he had this focus:

> It became obsessive, but now I've got the lid on it. I'm doing something positive about it. I think of her as somebody that I miss. Somebody that I've missed all these years. Miss the contact. Missed even seeing her as a baby and I think that was totally unfair. I'm now 57. I've lost a lot of friends of my own age and younger. My biggest regret is that I should have done it years ago.
>
> I asked Malcolm what he would like to say to Karen if they met.
>
> > That's a difficult question isn't it? To say that I would have loved her. That she was my daughter. That I didn't want her to be adopted. Always felt very hurt and let down by the fact that she was adopted. That I hope that she's had a happy life and that her adoptive parents loved her and wanted her – which her own parents did. I would like Karen, if she's not aware of it, to know the proper story of why she was adopted. To apologise. To say I have carried on loving her.

Finally, in this discussion of motives for contact, there is a group of eight men who explicitly wished to have a relationship with their child.

The Wish for a Relationship

As to his reasons for contact, one man said it was '…to reassure myself that he's ok. To find out about him. Could we have a relationship? I think that there must be some Karmic connection between us'. One man hoped that it might not be too late to have a relationship with his son:

I want to let him know that it's not that I didnae want him. I always have and always will love him. That I would like to, if possible, be part of his life. I would like to know where he's staying. He's not too old. There's things that I could do with him. I'm not too old.

The motives of four men were put in explicit parent-child terms: 'Why contact? The fact that she is my daughter. The fact that she is my flesh and blood. She has got a step-sister and step-brother'. This man was also clear about the specific nature of this relationship: 'I think of June (not the adopted child) as a second daughter. Sheila even if she came back, I'll never be her father. I'm her father biologically. I would accept that'. Another (who has had contact with his child) put it thus: 'I think the dad part is very difficult because she's had a dad that she respects. She tells people that I'm her dad. But I'm not her dad'. Another also couched his ambivalence in terms of regret: 'I missed out on her growing up. You wouldn't expect them to love you like a father but still...'

The men who shared their thoughts regarding this question of the difference between being a father (biologically) and a 'dad' (socially) seemed to be clear about the distinction. I could find no expressions of any impulse to replace an existing (adoptive) father, although one man came near to such a feeling of possessiveness. After saying that he always replied in the negative when asked whether he had children, he elaborated: 'The simple reason is that she's not mine at this moment in time. At this moment in time – probably the wrong thing to say – she's on loan to someone else'. However, this was qualified in the next sentence: 'I can't turn round and say she's mine because I've never met the girl. Although technically, in one sense, she is mine. On the other hand she isn't mine'. The facts are that the aspirations for connection and the offer of a quasi-paternal relationship with their child are a powerful set of hopes and a measure of the strength of the bond (albeit without the knowledge of the child) that these men feel in respect of their child.

The men's distinction between the two parental roles and responsibilities does not confirm the findings of the 1988 North American study of birth fathers. This study found that 'search activity was highly associated with serious thoughts of taking the child back' (Deykin *et al.* 1988, p.244). Based on this finding, Mullender and Kearn have voiced a need for 'caution' regarding birth fathers' involvement in the adoption process (1997, p.21). They acknowledge that there were biases in the North American study (derived from the fact that the interviewees were members of a campaigning group) but, notwithstanding this reservation, suggest that whilst the involvement of birth fathers in the adoption decision-making process is important, there may be a need to 'exercise care about involving them at later stages once an adoption has taken place' (*ibid.*). Presumably this comment is derived from the study finding that suggests that birth fathers may use any such contact opportunities as an occasion to 'retrieve' (*ibid.*) the child. The views and motivations for contact of the men in this study do not uphold such an apprehension and practitioners should therefore reconsider any reservations that automatically single out birth fathers for treatment with caution.

The aspirations to later-life contact and the more active searching of some of the men raise a question of ethics and policy. Arguments against the provision of information to birth parents about their children have included the notion that birth parents might disrupt the lives of the adopted person and their family (Field 1991; Trinder 2000). What were the men's attitude to information that might identify their sons and daughters?

Attitudes to Access to Identifying Information

The question of birth parent access to information about the adopted child is under debate (*Counter Blast* BBC2, 14 June 1999; Trinder 2000). Three main positions have emerged. There is the stance of many UK local authorities which will provide information only pertaining to the child's settling-in in the weeks and months after the adoption and nothing more (*Community Care,*

27 August, 1998). Then there exists a more 'open-the-books' argument modelled on Australian and New Zealand legislation (Field 1991). This provides for access to identifying information by all parties (Natural Parents Support Group 1993). Finally, there is a view that identifying information should be made available but only via trained post-adoption professionals who would act as mediators (Feast 1998). The UK Government has finally entered the debate by publishing guidelines about how adoption records holders might respond to birth relatives' requests for information and contact with adopted people (DoH 2000c). These guidelines are not mandatory.

Given this debate on greater openness as regards adoption records, all the men were asked for their views on birth parents' access to information about the child and specific details that would allow them to search for and contact their child, e.g. access to their children's adoptive names. Twenty were in favour of greater information relating to the adopted child. Seven men were against this and three said that they could not be categorical.

The notion that identifying information might be used by birth fathers to make unwanted interventions in their child's life has been expressed in Mullender and Kearn (1997, p.21). As noted previously, their reservations regarding birth father involvement in adoption proceedings are derived from the North American birth father research. However the attitudes of the men in this current study do not support reservations to the effect that, provided with the right information, birth fathers might seek to physically reclaim the child or somehow usurp the adoptive father. Of the 20 men who were in favour of access to identifying information, only one man said that, because he was her father, 'It was totally outrageous' that he could be denied information and the possibility of access to his daughter. A second man felt that he 'should have the same rights to know where she is'. By this he meant the ability to have access to his daughter's adoptive name and thus the opportunity to trace her. The other 18 men who were in favour of access to identifying information qualified their support for this: 'Yes. But I should not have the right to go up to her door and say "I'm her father". I should have the right to send a letter'. Most of those in favour of access to information (with the potential for contact) supported the adopted person's right to privacy. Any contact should be arranged through an intermediary so that 'the child can refuse'. It would be 'disruptive if birth parents were to have direct access'. Another man said, 'Yes but via mediation. You should have the right to know if they're still alive'. A number of others had a concern for the adoptive parents. Three men were undecided about overtures to contact, however they repeated the same sentiments of concern for the child and adoptive family: 'Depends on the circumstances. You should sound out the child first'.

The seven men who were *not* in favour of access to identifying information held similar considerations for the child and its adoptive family. These considerations outweighed the feelings and any potential rights of birth parents. One said, 'No. Birth parents could destroy a child's life. There should be well-publicised contact registers'. Another of those who disagreed with the idea of access to information said: 'The main thing is protection of the child. You should have the right to discuss with the authorities if the child is alive and well and happy'. These attitudes were spread evenly throughout both groups of men: those who had had contact and those who had not. Those who had not had contact were no more likely to be in favour of unqualified access to identifying information than those who had met their children.

The men's feelings about contact were similar to those of birth mothers who 'did not want to rock the boat' or disrupt lives (Bouchier *et al.* 1991, p.112). There was congruence with the attitudes of birth mothers who would like the right to information and the possibility of some form of indirect communication regarding the child's welfare (Wells 1994). The present activity of some birth parents and some of the birth fathers in this study, buying adoption certificates (not possible in Scotland) and hiring private detectives suggests that rather than *whether* birth parents should seek contact with their adopted children, the situation might require the more pragmatic response – a discussion of *how* these efforts are to be regulated. This should go alongside better promotion of the ACRs (Mullender and Kearn 1997). The consistent presence of concern for the adopted person and their family challenges any stereotypes that portray birth parent wishes for contact as somehow predatory. The discussion of access to information and mediation naturally concluded with the question of support services for birth fathers.

Support Groups for Birth Fathers

I invited the men to say whether they would use a support group for birth fathers. One man already ran such a group and another attended one. Sixteen said that they would use a support group. Among the reasons were statements such as: 'We don't talk enough about these things', 'to find out others' experiences and prepare for contact', 'to ease your pain'. In the words of another: 'I never spoke about it to anyone then, know what I'm saying, but this is great talking to you about it. I don't have anyone that I can really talk to'.

The main reasons for a support group were a need to share information, feelings and experiences. This finding is relevant to professionals involved in post-adoption services. However the ease with which the men could speak about their need for support only emerged towards the end of a lengthy and emotionally engaging interview in which considerable pains had been taken to establish rapport and encourage frankness. This suggests that if birth fathers are to be reached then gender specific efforts need to be made, as distinct from general invitations to birth parents to attend support groups (open to all) which tend not to be successful in attracting birth fathers. But what happened when the men's life-long hopes for a meeting with their child were realised?

Contact and Meeting

The ages of the ten men who had met their children ranged from one man who was in his early forties when his 17-year-old daughter traced him to another who was in his mid fifties when he found his daughter. On average the men were in their mid forties. The ages of their children at first contact was equally diverse, ranging from a 36-year-woman to the 17-year-old mentioned above. The children were an average age of 27 years old when they and their birth fathers met. As noted earlier, the length of time between having met and being interviewed was nearly three years, with the shortest being a meeting between one man and his son that had taken place six months before. The lengthiest time since meeting and interview was six years. Eight birth fathers and their daughters had met. The other birth fathers had met with sons.

The settings and the parties involved in these meetings varied. One man criticised the social worker for being present throughout the meeting and also for indicating that she felt 'time was up' after an hour. As he said, 40 years was a bit much to try to cram into 60 minutes. Another man arranged to meet his son at the son's place of work at lunch-time; the son brought a friend (who had also been adopted). Another man and his daughter met in the foyer of a hotel and were soon after joined by her adoptive parents and other adoptive relatives. Another man took his (adult) son to meet his adopted daughter who in turn had brought her husband and their child; they all met in an amusement park. One man's meeting with his daughter took place at his house where they were joined by a number of relatives and friends. In the last case the first contact from the adopted person had come from 'out of the blue' and the meeting took place two days afterwards.

These ten meetings and ensuing relationships do not provide sufficient information to draw conclusions regarding the shifting father-child dynamics and roles in the unique configuration brought about by adoption and subsequent contact. Birth father and adopted child contacts and relationships warrant a study in themselves. However, in light of the fact that neither of the two existing studies of birth fathers explores experiences of contact and relationships with adult children, what follows provides a starting point for further enquiry.

The Meeting

The ten men involved were asked two main questions. First, once it had been set up, what were their experiences of the first contact and meeting? For all of them the first meeting was an emotionally charged event. All ten of the meetings went very well; there was 'relief at how easy we communicated and how understanding she appeared' and pleasure because 'we hit it off'. For another man, there was 'delight' when his son began their first conversation with the observation that he was now owed 20 plus years pocket money, then: 'We sat and drank and talked until 5am then I put him to bed'. There was also shock:

> When she came in, oh my God, as soon as she came in, she was the double of her mother (signalled tears). We held each other and that was it, we sat down and started blethering...

For others there was a certain stupefaction:

> It was something I had been waiting for all my life. I was on a different plane, I was just still vacant. I was wandering about saying 'What's happening here?' And really that's what I think I was saying to myself – 'What's happening here?' To take the enormity of it was so much.

And there was the pleasure of recognition: 'I recognised her before she came into the hotel. I saw her walking along. I knew it was her 'cause she looks like me in many ways. And that's my daughter'. Another man said that the meeting felt like the arrival of the 'prodigal son'. Most of them recounted these events with passion and deep emotion. They were moved to tears.

The course of the first meeting was typically lengthy. They had sat up talking for hours: 'It felt just right' and 'There was a relief at how easily we communicated'. Irrespective of the amount of preparation beforehand, these first meetings were said to have gone well. For many of the ten men this first meeting provided an outlet for long-held feelings; the attainment of 'forgiveness' was mentioned by one. For another 'a big hole had been filled in my life'. 'All those years of waiting were over' and 'The worries had gone', said two other like-minded men. Here there is a verification of one of the motives for contact that was discussed earlier, namely the resolution of inner needs.

A second question invited the men to assess the nature of their relationship with their child. All but one of the men appeared to have established positive relations, expressed much pleasure with these and all referred to their son or daughter in a parental capacity: 'I love her as a daughter. There's no two ways about that. She is my daughter. My blood daughter'. Others gave similar responses: 'She's my babbie'; 'as father to son – I am living on through him'; 'Dat's my girl'. One man proudly quoted references by his son to him as 'my old man', another said that he felt pride at being referred to as the 'granddad' of his birth daughter's baby.

The man for whom the relationship had not developed spent hours describing how it had 'deteriorated spectacularly' until he felt he was 'gazing into the pit'. His daughter had traced him; he had married the birth mother and both he and she had remained together since the adoption. His account described what he regarded as 'being taken advantage of' – within a number of weeks his daughter had placed her children in his care whilst she went on holiday abroad. The man barely knew his grandchildren and had felt used. There were other occasions when her behaviour towards him seemed to jar and he had felt some hostility from her. His daughter's feelings and behaviour (conscious or otherwise) on discovering that her birth mother and birth father had married and parented other children a few months after her adoption can only be speculated upon. Also this man's account is, of course, only one interpretation of the dynamics of the contact.

Despite what had been a painful and protracted breakdown in their relationship, the birth father in question felt that there was 'always a roof for her'. He would not have wished to have been denied the possibility of meeting his daughter, after all, it was something he had 'been waiting for all my life'. For him, rejection and resolution co-exist in the achievement of contact. This last, and apparently 'failed' contact, seemed to be on course for re-establishment on a less acrimonious footing because at the time of the interview the daughter had begun to communicate with the man again (this time by letter and from the USA). The relationships that commenced and continued in euphoric mode, were not always strife-free. In six some element of discord had appeared but it was felt that this was part of getting to know a stranger – with whom the men were intimately linked.

All felt an intimacy, from the first point of contact, for a person that many of the men had never seen as a baby and none had seen since the birth. The men talked fondly of such activities as going to the pub with their son, their daughter's career and educational achievements; there was a feeling of closeness during their first telephone calls when long excited conversations took place. One man spoke proudly of being his daughter's confidante. One man said of his son that he now felt 'a concern for him', another that he was pleased and that everything was good and better than it should be: 'He's my only boy'. Typically, they spoke of 'hitting it off from the word go', with one man feeling a 'natu-ralness' about his first meeting with his son. Four men also reported a sense of pride. Some discovered that they were grand-fathers and had therefore had to alter the dates in their life history when they believed themselves to have first become so. Births of grandchildren (children of the adopted child) had predated those of their other (not adopted) children. In other words they had become grandfathers years earlier than they thought. One man was surprised to hear that he was a great grandfather.

Those who were contacted unexpectedly had different dilemmas than those whose search activity had been family knowledge. For these four men the adoption had not been a matter of common knowledge among those close to them. Despite it never having been a secret from those with whom they were closest, e.g. wives, some had not told their other children. Three men found themselves in the position of having to explain to a son or daughter that they were not, contrary to what had been understood, the man's eldest child. For these men, contact was not something that had been actively considered despite them having talked of the child as being regularly in their thoughts. Further research amongst those fathers that have not actively indicated a wish for contact but are 'found' would be necessary to explore the dynamics and reactions involved in this particular type of encounter.

The majority of the group of ten men with contact experienced improved self-esteem. As six of this group had indicated a willingness to be contacted or were those who had successfully traced their children, this is not surprising; an important quest had been concluded. One man said that since meeting with his child he had 'been able to get my life together'. In addition to the pleasure of contact, a number of men referred to a lack of resolution of other feelings. For one man, his feelings of guilt were not banished by the initiation of a relationship: 'There is no difference in the feelings that I have for her and those I have for my other children, except the guilt is still there'. A similar tension also appeared in one man's otherwise positive account of his meeting and relationship with his daughter. His report conveyed a sense of euphoria as a result of having successfully traced her six years previously. He now had contact with the birth mothers' parents, his (adopted) daughter, her husband and numerous grandchildren. Yet towards the end of the interview he said that 'Xmas is a bad time for me'. Such feelings contrast with others of pleasure and the successful establishment of relationships and suggest that the less altruistic aspect of the motive to search may not find a resolution in contact with the child.

The appearance of the birth father in the adoptive family, whether as a result of the adopted person's actions or those of the birth father, raises the question of kinship ties. Which is more real – kinship legally and socially formed by adoption or biological kinship created by 'blood' and genetics? Or does it have to be one or the other?[2]

Status and Terminology – Two Fathers?

On the question of the difference between themselves and the adoptive father, the majority of the men were clear: they might be 'the father' but the child's adoptive father was 'her dad'. They expressed a concern for the feelings of the adoptive parents:

> When I met him, I told him, yes, I was his father, but I wasn't his dad. His dad is the man who brings him up, and cuddles him when he's sick and tells him stories. Oh yeh, I was his father but I wasn't his dad.

During contact and subsequent meetings the question of the precise nature of the relationship arose. Many of the men had never seen the child at all yet they had feelings of fatherhood. They felt the same towards the child as they did towards their other (subsequent) children. For some, such thoughts and feelings had always been present since the adoption. For other men, feelings had emerged or grown in the years following the adoption. Notwithstanding feeling like a father, almost all the men expressed concern not to disrupt the relationship between the child and his/her adoptive parents. This was shown in the

---

2   There are other more prosaic challenges brought about by contact and the establishment of a relationship between the birth father and his child. These include the sudden growth of festive and birthday card lists and how to sign a letter, attendance (or not) at future births/christenings, marriages and funerals (and where to position oneself during these events – outside or inside? Front row or at the back?).

care taken to differentiate themselves (father) from the adoptive fathers ('dad'). In the words of one man, the adoptive father was 'the one that brought her up'. Another, who had met twice with his son, was cautious about their relationship especially *vis-à-vis* the son's parents. He 'did not want to come between him and his adoptive parents'.

In some cases, though, there were indications that the two roles of biological and social father were converging during contact and the subsequent relationship with the adopted child. Parent-child type social relations had begun to develop irrespective of whether the social (adoptive) father was a reality in the life of the adopted person. For example, a number of men talked of being called 'dad' or 'her real dad'. One man was asked to provide paternal advice and guidance regarding his daughter's choice of boyfriend. Another had been pleased to discover he had become a grandfather and after a while had gone on to baby-sit his daughter's children. Another had undertaken some business with his daughter's husband, who now regarded him as a father-in-law. And, as noted above, one man (whose contact with his daughter was not thought to have been positive) was clear that should the need arise 'there would always be a roof over her head' in his house.

Finch and Mason describe three key areas of filial obligation: personal care, financial support and accommodation (1991). There is some evidence of all three categories in the accounts. One man who had undergone a major heart operation was visited immediately afterwards and cared for by the daughter with whom he had only recently had contact. The case of one man who had unsuccessfully sought his son indicates that a parental role could extend to financial matters: 'We have got to make a will in a couple of week's time. Obviously if he is not here then he won't be in it'.

Yet, whilst these relationships are forming, a 'first' social father – the adoptive father – is already in existence. One of the birth fathers graphically conveyed this conundrum and the potential for a confusion of roles when asked how he thought his daughter regarded their relationship:

> Like the dad that she can tell everything to. I'm the one that doesn't give rows and judge and what not. The one that won't be shocked. The confidant. She seeks my approval. She won't get that from her adoptive mum and dad.

The little data that has emerged here does not refute indications from a study that explored contact and subsequent relationships from the adopted person's perspective (March 1995) in which it was found that some 'adoptees had engaged in "parent-child interactions"' (p.108). Modell has noted an aspiration to quasi-parent status among a campaigning group of American birth parents. CUB (Concerned United Birthparents), Modell suggests, holds the view that 'the birthparent contributes love and emotion, spontaneity and support to an existing parent-child relationship, in the manner of the divorced parent or fond uncle in American culture' (1986, p.658).

Going by what some of the men have recounted, there may very well be some new configuration of social roles emerging in these contacts with their children. Thus, birth parent expressions of hope or fantasy regarding 'equal status' with the adoptive parent (Modell *ibid.*) may be being fulfilled. At least two individual dynamics appear to converge in the men's reports. First, the men's feeling of connection to the child; this bond has survived an apparently insurmountable obstacle: the lack of someone to father. The expressions of care, a sense of obligation, and in some cases a feeling of fatherhood towards their children, indicated a wish to be someone in the child's life. This could embody a 'pull' to parent. Second, included in the adopted person's motives for seeking contact, there may be an element that complements the birth father's wish for a relationship. This is not to imply that the adopted person is seeking a father replacement; there is insufficient data relating to the search activities and motives of the children who found their fathers and from the men's accounts to suggest this. Additionally, there do not appear to be any great gaps or losses relating to fathering in the lives of the children who traced them.

The research also indicates that adopted people do not search or seek contact as a means of achieving a substitute parent (Howe and Feast 2000; Triseliotis 1977). However, Modell suggests the searches of adopted people may indicate an engagement in a re-interpretation of their own kinship (1994, p.12). The psychology of the adopted person's search could therefore incorporate the notion of the existence (or establishment) of a wider kinship network, i.e. one that includes two fathers (and two mothers, and for that matter additional siblings be they half or fully related to them). In the words of one adopted person who had recently met his birth father: 'Maybe one day "dad" will be more appropriate' (Post-Adoption Social Workers Group 1987, p.11). Perhaps then a parental role for the birth father may be ascribed by the child (now adult). His/her search activities, their initiation of contact and their feelings regarding the search for a birth father may be instrumental in the creation of another – second – father or father-like figure.

Thus there may be a chemistry at work in the meeting and subsequent relationship between birth father and child. This may have the effect of creating two different people or more accurately, two people each with a new social role acquired by virtue of their contact with each other. For the birth father, the new social role of father in respect of the adopted child, and for the adopted person, someone who now has a social relationship with a 'new' (or second) father. Not only may these social roles of a father and daughter/son come into being, the possibility of a multitude of other new roles is also a reality. Two men 'became' grandfathers at the first meeting between themselves and their children. Not only will they have acquired grandchildren but also these grandchildren acquired grandfathers. The list of those that are theoretically affected and involved is as numerous as the members of the two kin 'groups' that come together when contact takes place between a birth father and his adopted child.

The assumption or acquisition of a quasi-parenting role in relation to someone with whom the men have had no social parenting experience would seem to pose theoretical grounds for conflict. However none of the birth fathers reported conflict arising in their relations (where these were in existence) with the adoptive parents of the child. The position of stepfathers provides a precedent for behaviour and role negotiations in a situation where two social fathers co-exist. However stepfathers do not bring with them the symbolism that is manifest in such terms as 'natural father' (or, even more loaded, 'real dad') and the existence of a unique genetic connection. These potential rivalries have often been expressed in fiction.[3]

One thing is clear: in the men's accounts of their emerging relationships, transactions were taking place for which there was no blueprint. Exchanges were occurring on a social, emotional and material level for which there were no 'cultural rules' (Finch and Mason 1990, p.221). In their discussion of changes in the patterns of divorce and remarriage, Finch and Mason conclude that: 'There is a sense in which cultural rules to meet these situations are currently being written...' (*ibid.* p.244). A similar process of events developing a protocol of their own seems to be the case in these contacts between birth fathers and their children. This it would seem is a matter of great interest not only to social anthropologists but to all those who are concerned with how 'blended' families adapt and survive (Pill 1990).

---

3 In George Eliot's *Silas Marner*, the biological father who rejected the child as a baby rests his claim for custody of the child (now a teenager) against the child's adoptive father solely on the basis of his being the child's 'real' father. Irrespective of the life-long parent-child bond between the child and her adoptive parent, the biological father's case is given merit because of his being the 'natural' father.

This discussion of birth fathers, their wish for contact and the ramifications of their relationships with their children raises the issue of the usage and meaning of such terms as father, 'dad' and fatherhood. Conventional understandings of the status of father, what constitutes being a father and the meanings that may be attached to phrases such as 'dad' and 'father', are complicated by the men's experiences. In one sense there have always been two fathers. The other parties involved in adoption (the adopted person, the birth mother, adoptive parents and social workers) formally acknowledge this and are, generally, aware of it as a biological or genetic fact. The hands-on social parenting role undertaken by the adoptive father confers upon him the status of father and, as conventionally understood, he is the only man who experiences thoughts and feelings of fatherhood toward the child. In this sense the adoptive father occupies and fulfils the male parental role.

However, in exploring the narratives of the men in this study a second set of thoughts (and experiences) of fatherhood has been found – that of the birth father. In these few relationships between the child and his/her birth father, paternal-like activity has appeared not to be problematic, at least for the birth father. In the case of the men that have established relationships with their son or daughter, their long-held attachment to their child is now a matter for expression and testing in practice. Modell remarks that 'There is no obvious role for a birthparent in an American kinship system' (1986, p.658). The emergent roles in these 'father'-child relationships are intriguing events unfolding in society. The research community, policy-makers and, as we shall see, professional practitioners, have yet to catch up with this.

The narratives of these birth fathers continue but the interviews had to stop somewhere. From the vantage point of the present day – with or without contact with their child – what can be said about their experiences?

Emergent Themes in the Meaning of Contact

Two themes arising from this discussion of contact and hoped-for contact have already been drawn out. First, the men's attitude to contact with their adopted children has been shown to be primarily one of the need to know how the child has fared. This and other motives for contact have been circumscribed by the belief that the lives of the child and its adoptive parents should not be disrupted. A consensus was that any initial contact should be handled by professional mediators. Second, in the event of any meeting and possible subsequent relationship, the men were clear about their role as biological father and not 'dad'. The reality of life in these new family configurations will need more research and discussion. Undeniably, understanding of these new social situations has yet to catch up with the growing reality of the increase of meetings between adopted people and their birth parents.

There were two other major themes to emerge. The first arises directly from the men's accounts and is of immediate relevance to practitioners.

The Terminology of Reunion

For those involved in later-life searching and contact involving adopted people and birth parents there is the matter of how these meetings and subsequent relationships are to be termed. Post-adoption contact between birth mothers and their children has been referred to as 'reunions'. In publications for or concerning adopted people and their motivations for contact, 'reunion' is also the term typically employed for the contact between adopted people and their birth parents. For instance: *Preparing For Reunion* (Feast 1994; Feast *et al.* 1998), *Reunions: True Stories of Adoptees' Meetings with their Natural Parents* (Iredale 1997), *Adoption, Search and Reunion* (Howe and Feast 2000) and *Heart of the Reunion* (McMillan and Irving 1997). Mullender and Kearn also use the word 'reunion' to describe birth parents' aspiration for contact with their children (1997, p.20). March also uncritically uses the term 'reunion' in discussing the motivations of adopted people in their search for birth parents (1995, p.48). 'Reunion' has possibly entered into general use from the birth mother literature in which the imagery conveys the depth of the distress and pain that is felt by many birth mothers. This is graphically expressed in birth mother accounts of, for example, being prevented from breast feeding or cuddling their baby. The word carries with it not only the implicit message that two people who have once been united have met again, but that this meeting is the resolution of an interrupted process and that there will henceforth be a union of the two. The sub-text suggests the physical reunion of mother with the baby/child that she carried; two people brought together again after having been physically parted at birth.

This theme has tended to construct the terminology for all parties involved in later-life contacts. This study obviously could not deal with the physical effects of pregnancy and childbirth on the men. In their reports there were other less bodily expressions of a connection between them and their children. The connectedness that many of them felt was a state of mind. They tended not to use the term 'reunion' as regards contact or their hoped-for contact with the child. Instead, they spoke of seeking a meeting and in some cases, they hoped for a relationship. However, the contrary is the case according to the birth mother/adopted person literature. May there then be a gender difference here? Until this is further explored, it is suggested that the word 'reunion', whilst capturing certain of the hopes and feelings of birth mothers, may not be the most helpful way for professionals and others to describe meetings and contact between any of the parties involved.

The second emergent theme is of significance to everyone involved in adoption but is also important to all those concerned with fathers and their separation from their children. What is now offered is a theoretical framework for understanding the pain that fathers may feel when they are substantively apart from or bereft of their children.

Birthfathers and Attachment

The central thread that runs through the men's motivations for contact is that their child has remained in mind. A number of them believe that their status as a father to the child had never been relinquished. Such thoughts take on practical expression in later-life contact and the formation of relationships. Empirical evidence of affectional bonds has been found in the accounts of the birth fathers in this study. On two counts this is worth discussing further. First, because the presence of bonds or feelings of attachment in birth fathers is an original finding and, second, because attachment theory is used throughout the welfare professions and, in particular, the field of adoption. A finding of its relevance to fathers would be a significant development for work with men, especially young fathers-to-be.

Attachment theory has its origins in the work of John Bowlby (1969, 1973, 1980) and Mary Ainsworth (1969); its focus is the infant and how, in its interactions with a main caregiver, the child develops an attachment towards the caregiver (Bretherton 1991). The child-specific quality of this attachment differs from the attachments that adults form in that the relationship between the child and its attachment figure is that of care receiver to caregiver. Caregiving includes ingredients that, generally speaking, only a relatively helpless infant requires, such as feeding and protection. The child's attachment behaviour is triggered and exhibited whenever its attachment to the caregiver is threatened (Ainsworth 1969; Bowlby 1969).

Attachment theory appears at first sight to offer little help in an exploration of how the birth fathers in this study have come to feel a bond with their child. This is because of its focus upon the child and, predominantly, the child's interactions with its mother, there being an absence of a focus on fathers in the literature (Howe 1995). An additional limitation of attachment theory is that it is empirically driven – it rests on observable behaviour (Bowlby 1984, p.3). On this basis, an explanation of how birth fathers in adoption may make and hold attachments to absent children is not obviously apparent in traditional theories of attachment.

However some writers have argued that attachment theory can be used to explain how adults also make attachments. Whilst not the same as the specific attachment that an infant may form (Rutter 1995), the process by which attachments are made in adulthood may have commonalities with that of infant-primary caregiver attachment (Ainsworth, 1991; Bowlby 1979; Weiss 1991). Interest in how adult attachments may be formed is growing (Crowell and Treboux 1995) and there have been calls for further research (Ainsworth 1991; Rutter 1995; Weiss 1991). However, there appears to be nothing in the literature on adult attachment that concerns the process of how *paternal* attachment may occur. Despite this research gap, the concept of 'bonds formation' in attachment theory is worth utilising for an explanation as to how the birth fathers in this study have come to feel the way that they do about their children. In addition, an understanding of early paternal attachment would have considerable relevance for all expectant and new fathers and those who work with them.

To distinguish between infant attachment and that of parents to their children, the term 'bonds' is often used (Ainsworth 1991; Fahlberg 1991). Bowlby (1979) used the phrase 'affectional bonds' to describe the connections that adults may develop with each other (Ainsworth 1991). Weiss uses the phrases 'attachment bond' and 'attachment relationship' to make a similar distinction between the bonds that adults form and the attachment formation process that is unique to infants (1991, p.75). However, as Ainsworth notes: 'We still know remarkably little about the processes involved in the formation and maintenance of the bond, or even the criteria that mark its establishment' (1991, p.40). Whilst writers on attachment theory have looked at the parental bonding process and suggested that this may begin pre-birth, usually the focus has been the mother (Fahlberg 1991, p.20). Howe also raises the possibility of bond formation before social interaction when he refers to: 'Many developmental psychologists (who) believe that parents, too, are biologically disposed to bond with their child...' (1995, p.52).

In his exploration of the 'bonds of adult attachment' Weiss usefully concludes that:

> The development of parental attachment to immature children seems to occur suddenly and to persist strongly. Unsystematic observation and interview suggest that adults who may have no sensed need for a relationship with children for many years may, in a very brief time, develop very strong investment in newly born children. Loss of a child seems regularly to give rise to a state of grief in which separation protest is intermeshed with protection drives. This state is remarkable for its persistence. (1991, p.74)

Here, Weiss is referring to the feelings of parents whose child has died at or soon after birth. Neither Howe nor Weiss make it explicit as to whether they include fathers in their reference to parental bonding. However Ainsworth has extended the discussion by addressing bonding and the paternal experience: 'The tendency has been to consider the bond of father to child as somehow less deeply rooted than the bond of mother to child'. She then asks: 'Does paternal behaviour have the same kind of biological underpinning as maternal behaviour?' (1991, p.40).

Furthermore Ainsworth usefully shifts the focus from any interaction between those who may bond with each other (either pre- or immediately post-birth) to the *individual who experiences the sense of a bond* (1991, p.37; emphasis added). She suggests that: 'Relationships are dyadic, whereas affectional bonds are characteristic of the individual', and goes on to describe how a bond may be manifested in the individual:

> In an affectional bond there is a desire to maintain closeness to the partner. In older children and adults that closeness may to some extent be sustained over time and distance and during absences, but nevertheless there is at least an intermittent desire to re-establish proximity and interaction and usually pleasure – often joy – upon reunion. Inexplicable separation tends to cause distress and permanent loss would cause grief. (1991, pp.37–38)

According to Ainsworth then, a bond can be an individual experience that may be felt in absentia, i.e. without the presence of the other party. This, and the above discussion of a possible paternal process of early attachment, suggest that a bond felt by a father for a child can be formed without social interaction and be sustained for years in the thoughts, emotions and psychology of the father. These developments in attachment theory and their references to adults who may experience separation, loss, grief and a hope for reunion with their 'lost' child, provide explanations for the behaviour and motivations of the birth fathers in this study. They also represent advances in the way that we think about expectant and new fathers in general.

To conclude this chapter and the chronological presentation and discussion of the men's adoption experiences, it can be said that certain distinct themes have emerged in the men's narratives. A central one is the presence of the child in mind and the existence of feelings of attachment, as discussed in this section. Also adoption has been shown to be 'a life-time condition' for the men in this study (Byrd Dean 1988, p.24; Feast 1994, p.157). And it has been shown that there are parallels with the experiences of birth mothers, e.g. in the men's attitudes to contact and access to information.

Crucially, there are the men's emotions and thoughts in respect of the adopted child. Despite these men having had no experience of day-to-day care and having never seen the child since its birth some 30 years previously (and in some cases not even this visual contact had taken place), the child remained in their minds. A bond with their adopted child seemed to run through these birth father's lives like the lettering in a stick of seaside rock – out of sight has not meant out of mind. This study has shown that a man's feelings and thoughts for his child may not necessarily be engendered by social care and activity alone. Despite being 'childless fathers' in Modell's sense (1994), many of the men in this study felt an affectional bond, which some described as a parental feeling, with the child. This bond exists in the absence of the type of behaviour and activity that is conventionally understood to be the basis for such a bond: social parenting activities such as the provision of nurture and care and mutual interaction and affection.

These birth father narratives have indeed 'yielded much more than the vacuum that previous authors have suggested exists' (Brinich 1990, p.59) and fatherhood has been shown to have more dimensions than has been imagined. How does this help us understand fathers as a whole and birth fathers in particular? What are the implications for policy-makers and practitioners?

Part III

Birth Father Narratives

The Implications

Chapter Nine

Understanding Men and Fathers

The extent to which people continue to feel personally and socially related to others from whom they have been separated for a lifetime, or whom they may never ever have seen, is one enigma posed again by the findings reported here. It would greatly repay further research. (Mullender and Kearn 1997, p.27)

This chapter discusses some of the more theoretical issues and questions that have been raised in the course of exploring birth fathers' experiences. It is argued that if men were judged to be fathers solely on their activities in respect of their children then the behaviours and emotions of the men in this study would be inexplicable. This study has brought to the fore a more affective dimension of fatherhood. This includes how men carry their child around with them in their minds. Light has been shed on men's self-perceptions of fatherhood. Given particular attention in this chapter are the processes by which men become fathers and, for the birth fathers in the study, the possible hows and whys in respect of a sense of fatherhood that has been retained for several decades without any parenting experience. The chapter also discusses how the study has been helpful in understanding men and their relation to fatherhood.

Being a father has been mainly defined as a set of social actions, e.g. active participation in parenting, the ability to provide nurture and raise an infant, being a male role model. 'Being there' has been a potent and controversial yardstick used to measure and judge what is deemed to be a good father or a bad father. In the case of young unmarried fathers, the ability to support a child in the financial sense of contributing towards upkeep has increasingly been what defines a 'good father' (Speak *et al.*1997). But while public and official definitions of fatherhood are under constant construction and opinions are being advanced, little remains known of the less functional aspects of being a father. Men's self-perceptions of fatherhood, where the role of fatherhood fits in a man's identity and the relevance of biological fatherhood to the formation of social fatherhood, are matters that are absent from both contemporary public discussion and research. This study, with its uncovering of men's hidden worlds – the secret set of emotions that relate to a baby once glimpsed if at all – has brought some light to the various debates. In one sense a modest claim would be that the stereotype of the absent and uncaring father (that if a child is out of sight it is out of mind for a man) has not been proved.

Many of the birth fathers in this study, whilst teenagers, cared for and felt an obligation to their unborn child and the birth mother – though some of this was unfulfilled. Some had had expectations of parenthood and family life and were opposed to the adoption. Others were in support of the adoption. For all of them the adoption was an emotionally salient event in their lives and almost all felt that their subsequent lives had been influenced by thoughts of their child. A considerable number of the men felt loss. Some defined themselves as fathers at the time and for them this belief in themselves as fathers (of the adopted child) had not ebbed since the adoption. For some of the birth fathers in this study, this part of their identity became stronger as life went on.

As discussed in the previous chapter, a central finding has been the evidence of a bond or 'bondedness' with the absent child, in most cases a child with whom there had been no more than one brief contact, if that. This therefore suggests that the mechanism of bonding with a child may be less gendered than we have imagined it to be; none of the conventional mechanisms for women and men (biological or social interaction factors) had been in place in the case of the men in this study. The finding of attachment amongst this group of fathers, who have only experienced the biological dimension of fatherhood, is a significant one. It indicates that fatherhood and men's perceptions of themselves as fathers may be formed under conditions that do not normally suggest its presence, i.e. where there has been no parenting and no contact with the child.

Research has shown that expectant fathers can feel a connection with their unborn child. In other specific instances, e.g. men absent as soldiers, a sense of fatherhood may continue after the birth without ever having seen the child (Bell 1943; Turner and Rennell 1995). However such studies involved men who were in expectation of a continuing relationship with their child. But, in the case of many of the men in this study, a sense of fatherhood appears to have continued for decades after the adoption, a process and event that officially ruled out the possibility of a relationship with their child. How could such enduring feelings of fatherhood exist?

The Strength of Blood Ties

Some of the men drew upon or quoted a belief in the primacy of blood to explain feelings such as responsibility for the child. Modell has researched and written on adoption and has drawn attention to the power of a belief in the strength of blood ties in Western societies. She refers to 'the significance of blood in American understandings of kinship' (1994, p.4). This belief is a powerful one in literature and culture, legislation regarding heritage (*ibid.* p.26), and in mythologies and beliefs: 'blood is thicker than water'. It will be recalled that some of the men drew on imagery that included blood when asked how they felt about their connection to the child. Others used phrases that denoted a similar physical connection between themselves and the child; they felt the child was part of them. There is evidence that adopted people have a strong belief in the significance of blood ties (Sachdev 1992, p.64). This then is paralleled in some of the men's strong beliefs in the connection signified by blood. Whilst such beliefs in the importance of blood ties may offer one explanation for the men's feelings of fatherhood, another school of thought suggests a biological factor.

A Psycho-Biological Connection

There is a small body of work on the psycho-biological elements that might contribute to the development of a consciousness of fatherhood. This posits a pre-birth process of becoming a father in which men may undergo perceptible psychological and biological changes in their transition to fatherhood *before* hands-on experience of parenting (Diamond 1995a, 1995b; Mackey 1985, 2001; Motluk 2000; Pleck 1995).

This process may commence with conception and continue throughout pregnancy, birth and afterwards. Mackey suggests that there is more to the ingredients of fatherhood than the act of conception and social activity with the child, that there is also a 'fathering instinct' and that the father-child bond has a genetic basis (1985, p.170). The research in this field has focused upon married fathers-to-be of all ages, not necessarily young expectant fathers. Overall there is a suggestion that there might exist a male equivalent of pregnancy that incorporates the development of a material connection with the child, albeit less physically experienced than in the case of women. In a similar vein Cohen argues that men's consciousness of fatherhood may begin before birth and the time when they can actively parent; for some men, such a process may begin in pregnancy and be 'broader and more dramatic' than is imagined (1993, p.10). Elsewhere, Krampe and

Fairweather's (1993) reference to an element of 'biological essence' to the fatherhood experience and the discovery of hormonal changes in expectant fathers (Berg and Wynne-Edwards 2001) suggest that there could be more at work than social activity in the formation of men's sense of fatherhood.

In the case of the men in this study, nearly all of them young men at the time of the pregnancy and birth, it seems that many developed a mental connection with the child. The unborn child became a presence in their minds – not unlike the process that has been described for other (more conventional) expectant fathers. Thoughts of the child did not 'evaporate' with or after the adoption. The man who felt 'rubbed out' legally but not emotionally seems to sum up their feelings.

Could the men's experiences therefore add weight to the notion of a genetic blueprint for fatherhood that takes shape in an expectant father's psychology and emotions? (Mackey, 1985, p.177). If so, it would seem to be remarkable for it to continue in place after such time and without the social stimulation of interaction with the child. The nine men who never parented a child that was biologically theirs after the adoption might indicate that there is indeed something working far below the surface, and this may relate to the consequences when such a blueprint to fatherhood is unfulfilled. Could there have been psycho-biological factors that kept these particular men from proceeding to fatherhood (again)? The matter of 'secondary infertility' (i.e. the inability to have children after the experience of adoption) has already been generally accepted in the birth mother literature (Deykin *et al.* 1984). The question of any 'paternal programme', i.e. a biological underpinning for fathers' behaviour referred to by Ainsworth (*op. cit.* 1991), that is assumed almost as a given for women, would be of great relevance to all those who work with male teenagers and young men.

Thoughts of the Child as Symbolic

Rather than explicable because of any adherence to societal belief systems or any psycho-biological element, the men's enduring sense of a connection to the child may have its roots in the circumstances of the adoption. Could it be that the child, in the mind's eye of many, may be representative of something else other than fatherhood, but not fully recognised? Is it possible that the child may be a symbol of unrequited love for the birth mother? A significant number of the men linked the birth mother and child in their accounts of loss; still others had a continued affection for the birth mother. The child may then be symbolic of unrealised hopes for a family life.

Thoughts of the child may also be symbolic of what for some, was a formative (because felt as emasculatory) experience. The men's perceived failure to assume responsibility, or resist the intervention of other authorities in the case of the adoption, and the consequent feelings of disenfranchisement which emerged for many, left deep impressions. These thoughts may then help form salient milestones in these birth fathers' mental life maps. Perhaps then, contact with the child is a route to self-healing and seen as an opportunity to discharge unpaid dues. Here then, thoughts of the child could be symbolic in that the child may have come to not only represent a burden unshouldered, but also thoughts of the child/adoption may have come to lodge in their minds as some kind of wrong that has gone unrighted.

The Men's Experiences of Being Parented

Finally, in this speculative exploration of the basis for the men's feelings of fatherhood, there may be influential events that long pre-date the birth and adoption, namely their own experiences of being fathered and parented. These experiences can be divided into at least two categories.

The Influence of a Father on a Birth Father

The first could be that the men's sense or model of fatherhood comes from the understandings that these men have about what constitutes a good father. For example, a good father does not (in the men's words) abandon a child. May such a belief be related to their positive experiences of being fathered or experiences of not being adequately fathered or parented? Could it be that the perpetuation of thoughts of the child is an expression of a concern to be a good father that is based upon their formative childhood experiences? Here there may be a process of historical continuity where it is possible to trace the influence of the fathers of men who have had a child adopted. Given the influence in general that fathers have on their sons (Andry 1962; Blendis 1982; Katz 1999; Morrison 1998), this would not be surprising.

Parental Loss and its Influence on a Birth Father

Second, it will be recalled that more than a quarter of the men had experienced some form of parental loss prior to the pregnancy. It may be that feelings of anxiety and distress regarding the adopted child are connected to much earlier personal needs, e.g. an unassuaged need for comfort and consolation arising from the loss of a parent. Perhaps for some of the birth fathers in this study, the pregnancy arose out of lives that were already somewhat disrupted? At some unconscious level, were they (when engaging in unprotected sexual intercourse) seeking a replacement family? Pannor (quoted in Barber 1975) suggests that 50 per cent of unmarried fathers have an absent or deceased father. Pannor *et al.* suggest that parental loss, whether through death or separation, could be a contributory factor in behaviour such as failure to take precautions in sexual relations. The need to prove oneself as a man may be more intense in someone who lacks a father, resulting in unconscious actions to prove manhood and boost self-esteem, e.g. by fathering children (1971, pp.125–128).

Therefore feelings of loss could pre-date the adoption process which in itself involved a number of losses: the child and a relationship with the birth mother. In the previous discussion it was suggested that the child may be symbolic of what could have been – perhaps family life. In the case of the birth fathers that underwent childhood or teenage loss of a parent, perhaps their present day feelings have roots in events *prior* to the adoption. These two ideas, involving the influence of experiences of being parented and parental loss, are as intriguing as the other possible explanations for the men's feelings of fatherhood and attachment to the child. Here too there is relevance for those who work with young men whose experiences of fathering and parenting has been poor, interrupted or non-existent.

Whether any one of the above explanations better fits than another, the fact of the matter is that for the men in this study, for most of their lives, this sense of fatherhood had no observable reality as far as the child was concerned. There were a few concrete indicators of the men's sense of a connection or bond with their child. Most men had registered on ACRs; some men were engaged in searching. Some men's social and emotional relations had been affected; they had not fathered or parented again, and they attributed poor mental health and disrupted relationships to the effects of having given up a child for adoption.

Overall, however, the attachment that the men have in respect of their children is one that can be mostly measured only in their thoughts and feelings. These birth father narratives consist of a combination of memories and responsibilities, curiosities and beliefs, processes begun and loves unrequited. All of these seem to have intertwined with each other to constitute the narratives of these birth fathers and explain their attachment to their children. This amounts to a non-conventional aspect of fatherhood made the more so by its capacity to exist in an apparent social vacuum: without the child. It appears that for many in the study a switch was thrown with news of a child of theirs – either at the time or later – out in the world. Across time and space this has not been reversed. In their minds they became fathers and have retained that bond with their child.

The next and final chapter discusses implications of the study findings; where the general needs of fathers and their children are at issue but also in the particular fields of social work with men and their families and adoption.

Chapter Ten

Working with Fathers

This study has uncovered a depth and variety in the experiences and identities of men who are birth fathers and brought an understanding to their enduring feelings about their children. In summary, we have seen how at the time of the adoption, 25 teenage men felt that they had been in a steady relationship. An exploration of the various stages and associated changes in the men's lives showed the impact of becoming fathers, the adoption and the way that they had come to feel about their child. We saw how feelings of fatherhood emerged and grew for a majority of the group and how only one fits the stereotype of an irresponsible young man who abandons a pregnant girl friend. Over a half of the men in the study were against the adoption of their child and it has been shown that 21 out of the 30 men underwent considerable distress in the weeks and months after the adoption. Also we have seen how the negative feelings arising from the experience of adoption cast a long shadow in their subsequent lives and relationships. For instance, nine of the men had no other children. Their child was rarely far from their thoughts, with feelings of parenthood, loss and concern for the child featuring prominently. Most of them had sought or offered contact with their adult child and 20 out of 30 were in favour of greater access to information about the child. In relation to the meetings that took place and relationships that formed, for all but one of ten men involved, these were said to be positive. Finally, it has been shown that the experiences of the birth fathers in this study have many similarities with those in studies of birth mothers.

It should be remembered that the men's adoption experiences relate to those of baby adoptions and that these are a much smaller proportion of today's adoptions. Men who have some experience of parenting a child that is adopted at an older age (and perhaps have contested that adoption) will obviously have a different set of experiences and thoughts than these men. It will also be recalled that the men had been reachable because of their contact with post-adoption services or displayed an interest in birth parent issues. Notwithstanding these considerations, the study offers everyone involved in working with men new understandings of the feelings and experiences of fathers.

Involving Fathers

The findings from the study may help repair the neglect to fathers in general and raise greater awareness of their feelings and their needs. Lewis notes that: 'There has been little serious discussion about what policy makers and service providers can actually do to support men's parenting' (2000, p.1). An appreciation of the complexities of fatherhood, particularly the notion of an affectional bond with the child existing either without ever having socially parented or no longer parenting, might go toward informing the discussion of the needs of fathers and their children.

The contribution that men may be capable of making to the task and role of being a parent may be deeper than has hitherto been imagined, and the widely accepted view that parenting is essentially the responsibility of mothers (Buckley 1998) is called into question. The attitude that children are, at the end of the day, women's work has negative consequences for all: men, women and children. This can been seen in the undervaluing of child care services and the lack of men in employment in primary schools, nursery work and family centres (Ghate *et al.* 2000). The National

Childbirth Trust and the National Family and Parenting Institute have also drawn attention to the lack of services for new fathers, e.g. restrictions on visiting hours that affect fathers who are at work. The same applies in children's welfare practice where meetings are routinely arranged during the day, thus making it difficult for working fathers to attend (Flouri and Buchanan 2001). Men's equal capacity to parent, and the need for this to be acknowledged in the interests of their children, remains to be universally accepted. The right to paternity leave has only recently been introduced in the UK and battles are still being waged about the flexibility of men's working hours.

The powerful societal preconceptions about young men in particular and their unwillingness to become and remain involved in the lives of their children are also called into question by this study's findings of young men who responded to the challenge of unexpected pregnancy. As previously discussed, the study's findings also challenge negative attitudes toward non-resident fathers and contribute to the debate over the legal position of unmarried fathers. At the time of writing, in relation to the rights and duties of parenthood, the law does not regard a child's mother and father as equals and there are no plans to alter the position of existing unmarried fathers (Pickford 1999). As signalled in the references to fathers and their children, it is difficult to consider fathers and fatherhood separately from children's welfare – especially with regard to social work practice and child protection.

Social Work Practice with Men

It might be assumed that professional attitudes and practice towards fathers has moved on since the 1960s and 70s however, research does not bear this out. In their review of social work literature, Grieff and Bailey (1990) draw attention to negative assumptions about fathers. They found an absence of discussion, unless the father's behaviour was a risk to children or a destructive influence in a family. March refers to a 'general disregard for fathers in the family literature' (1995, p.110). Research in the social services files of children in care has found 'a lack of information about fathers and the focus on mothers suggested that the contributions, positive or negative, which fathers make to their children's well-being were ignored' (Masson, Harrison and Pavlovic 1997, p.2). Edwards also cites evidence of health and social welfare practitioners' negative attitudes towards men (1998). It seems then that men's parenting is viewed as 'a social problem rather than a social strength' (Lewis 2000, p.9).

This attitude sharpens in the field of child protection practice – to the detriment of children. Trotter has drawn attention to professionals' emphasis upon the negative behaviour of men and has argued that men are only discussed when they are abusive parents. Non-abusing fathers, she suggests, have received less attention (1997). More recently, a review commissioned by the Department of Health found that:

> Non-resident fathers are minimally involved in the child protection process, but the studies contain several examples of how they can, or could, be involved and how they are a useful resource. (Ryan 2000, p.44)

Typically only one-third of non-resident fathers were included in the child protection process. Publication of this review of research and a major UK conference held in London in September 2001 (*My Dad, My Protector?* NSPCC/Fathers Direct) signal an advance in the discussion of the role that fathers can play in preventing abuse (Fatherwork Autumn 2001).

According to Daniel and Taylor (1999) gender bias can be traced throughout much of social work policy and practice. They suggest that stereotypes regarding men's inability to care and nurture are detrimental to men and, because these assumptions involve defining men and women in gender-restricted roles, women too are negatively affected. Therefore it would appear that at the beginning of the millennium, social work, because of its exclusion of fathers and predominantly single-minded focus on mothers, remains a gender biased profession. There are a number of practical implications that flow from this.

In its finding that birth fathers have an attachment to their child, this study is at one with one major piece of research on non-resident fathers. Bradshaw *et al.* (1999) found that, when contact was defined more widely than physically seeing a child, a father and child's relationship could be discerned through other media such as e-mail, fax and telephone. Thus they were able to identify a continuing connection between so-called 'absent fathers' and their children. Therefore a solid research base is emerging that challenges negative assumptions in respect of how fathers regard their relationship with their children. Absence of contact should not be assumed to mean indifference. In this vein there have been a number of articles in the UK press that have pointed out the difficulties faced by non-resident fathers in establishing and maintaining contact with their children (Deborah Orr, *The Independent*, 16 June 2000; Sue Summers, *The Observer*, 21 October 2001). Elsewhere it has been noted that court welfare officers have undervalued the role of fathers (Fatherwork Autumn 2001). The challenge is how to involve fathers rather than whether to.

Practice with young, unmarried fathers and fathers who are without custody and non-resident may be informed by such knowledge of fathers' capacity for paternal commitment in the absence of the child. Where there is a young unmarried expectant mother who cannot care for her child, there may also be a young father or his family who can provide it with a home in a family of origin. Where there is a young mother and child, there may be a young father who, simply because their relationship has failed or he has no means to participate in providing, cannot be discounted from a paternal relationship and connection, vital to both himself and his child:

> Perhaps, rather than focussing our attention on those fathers who do not wish to be involved, we should attend to supporting those who do, in both practical and psychological ways. We

might begin by removing the negative messages which poor press gives out and focussing attention on the many good examples of young men and young fathers. (Speak 2001)

In the knowledge now that there may be unexpressed bonds, workers in this field will have to explore new ways to 'invite in' young men.

Another neglected area of practice with a particularly isolated group of fathers who have little or no contact with their children consists of work with those who are in prison. A number of initiatives have begun that recognise the significance of maintaining links (where appropriate) between fathers in gaol and their children, for instance, the 'Long Distance Dads' programme sponsored by the National Fatherhood Initiative in the US. There is also news of UK work begun in Wandsworth Prison by the organisation 'Fathers Direct' (Fatherwork Summer 2001). These activities start from the basis of the welfare of both father and child.

Long-term feelings of grief were a feature of the lives of the men in this study. The existence of a connection with the unborn child and the capacity for grief when separated from it illuminates men's ability to be deeply moved by events such as still births, traditionally seen as an area where emotional support has been extended only to women. The fact that the men said that one of the instrumental reasons for divorce and separation was the negative effects of unacknowledged, long-held feelings of distress and loss might be borne in mind by couple counsellors (is there a hidden (lost) baby?). At least one man in the study said he had been surprised when his distress finally came out during counselling. Also, those practitioners who help parents who experience the death of a baby may wish to explore the father's particular sense of loss. Nearly a third of the men in the group attributed their failure or refusal to become parents to the effects of the adoption. Such secondary infertility in men would be an additional point of exploration for those involved with couples where becoming parents is a point of conflict.

This study's findings of thoughts of a child unseen also raises questions in the case of men who have been donors in assisted reproduction. In the event that children born by such methods ever gain the right to knowledge of their biological fathers (and therefore gain the possibility of tracing them), then it should be borne in mind that the feelings and experiences of such men may not be a million miles away from those of the birth fathers in this study.

Adoption Policy and Guidance

This study has shown that some birth fathers had wished to be key parties in the overall adoption process from birth to any subsequent post-adoption contact, and were denied this opportunity. A UK High Court judge has called for an examination of local authority procedures to clarify the rights of birth fathers in adoption (*Community Care*, 7 December 2000). Yet there is evidence that, as in the case of other areas of social welfare, views regarding the participation of men are mixed and knowledge of fathers may be based upon assumptions rather than fact.

Thirty-five years ago when Anglim made a plea for birth fathers to be included in adoption practice with birth mothers, she raised the question of the profession's avoidance of birth fathers (1965, p.340). In the same vein, Platts noted the existence of practitioner bias against birth fathers (1968), as did others that followed (Pannor *et al.* 1971). The accounts of the birth fathers in this study confirm that such bias existed in the UK throughout the period in question: the 1950s to the 1970s (with one man providing evidence of being marginalised in 1985). This is shown in their accounts of not being consulted or feeling unwanted – despite a willingness to be involved – and in some cases being actively excluded. Since the time of the men's adoption experiences it appears that little may have changed. Daniel and Taylor argue that a major text used in fostering and adoption practice (Fahlberg 1991) repeats the gender role assumptions contained in traditional attachment theory by focusing upon mothers to the exclusion of fathers. They argue that such assumptions are not so much explicitly expressed, but are shown by the absence of any references to fathers in particular, and the use in case examples of only women's experiences (1999).

A number of policy considerations flow from the discovery in this study that adoption happened to these men as well as to the birth mothers of the child. One is the manner in which birth parents are referred to in the official and professional literature. There has been a considerable increase in the US and the UK in the number of meetings and contacts between birth parents and their adopted children and research is underway into these emerging relationships (Howe and Feast 2000), or has already been published (Carsten 2000). This has tended to focus upon the adopted person's experiences. Knowledge of the potential social, interpersonal and inter-familial dynamics of meetings between birth parents (birth mothers and birth fathers) and adopted people from the perspective of birth parents will be vital for post-adoption policy and practice which is presently informed only by a very small research base. In relation to birth parents, this research base is composed of birth mother experiences only.

Understandably perhaps, publications have tended to reflect this disparity. Guidance issued in the not-so-distant past has not reflected the experiences outlined in this study. In a pamphlet for adoptive parents entitled *Talking About Origins* (BAAF 1984), whilst the birth mother is discussed there is no reference to birth father. More recently, a joint briefing from the Association of Directors of Social Work and British Agencies for Adoption and Fostering entitled 'What is adoption?' includes a paragraph on the changes in adoption compared to the position 20 or 30 years ago (ADSS-BAAF June 2000). This discusses adoptions that took place then as if there were no birth fathers and ends: 'Because of the substantial social changes during the past 30 years, fewer than 200 single mothers take that course of action today'.

Additionally, as previously pointed out, Government publications continue to either refer to birth parents in a generic sense (and really mean birth mothers) or birth mothers only (DoH 2000c). The one birth father who is mentioned in the latter publication is depicted as seeking contact because of his wife's needs, the birth mother, and not in his own right.

These omissions perpetuate the generalisation that adoptions only happen to women and recall the point made by Anglim regarding how professionals can contribute to 'a myth that suggests that a child born out of wedlock has only one natural parent' (1965, p.340). There were only ten meetings and relationships between the birth fathers in this current study and their children, so all we have is a snapshot of these experiences and the men's views. However this study, with its findings from both contact and non-contact experiences and the revelation that there are 1500 birth fathers on ACRs, suggests that any future literature should reflect this new knowledge of the existence and aspirations of birth fathers.

A second policy matter lies with the UK Government and relates to the relatively low number of birth fathers who use post-adoption services: ACRs and support groups. This stands in contrast to the experiences of the men in this (albeit small) study which suggests that many more men than we imagine would benefit from post-adoption advice and counselling, if they knew how to access these services. The ACRs should especially be publicised and it should be possible to devise particular advertisements that appeal to birth fathers, ones that emphasise the value to an adopted person of knowing both their maternal and paternal origins. However, should birth fathers seek to register on the UK Government-sponsored ACR for England and Wales they face a particular problem. This is the requirement that they can prove that they are the birth father of the adopted child in question, either by having signed the birth certificate or being referred to as the father in the adoption proceedings. This study has shown that whilst some of the birth fathers could provide this type of proof, many would not be in a position to, as there was no requirement that they sign any of the adoption papers. Furthermore many of the men in the study were excluded from the events and so were unlikely to be mentioned in any of the various papers and documents.

This requirement of proof of fatherhood effectively excludes what may be thousands of birth fathers from registering on the second largest ACR in the UK and therefore prevents adopted people from achieving full knowledge of their origins. This is particularly disadvantageous in cases where the birth father is the only one who is willing to register; either the birth mother may be deceased or she may not be in a position to offer contact. This study's findings of birth fathers' long-held commitment to their children and what they can offer should inform a review of the above policy which effectively hampers contact between adopted people and their birth fathers.

Third, personal experience suggests that birth fathers remain to be involved or represented in all aspects of adoption policy and practice, e.g. adoption panels and training for prospective adoptive parents. The findings of this study of birth fathers – from their willingness to be participate in the adoption process, to their wish for contact, including evidence of considerable post-adoption distress – hopefully demonstrate the importance of not excluding birth fathers from adoptions. This inclusion would not only be in cases involving their children, but also where a birth father perspective might be of value, e.g. in training social workers.

Adoption Practice both Pre and Post Placement

In the case of the men in this study, welfare and adoption workers clearly played decisive roles at the various junctures, perhaps not in the ultimate adoption decision, but without condemnatory attitudes the potential distress of the experience may have been minimised. A typical comment from the birth father was of not having had any choices laid out before them. An important consideration that emerges from these accounts is that, irrespective of whether an individual worker was seen as helpful, the sum effect of the attitudes of all welfare professionals, semi-professionals and others (secretaries, court officials), was felt to be hostile. Given the amount of distress experienced by the men in this study, adoption practitioners are advised to re-consider any assumptions that may be made about the relative 'strength' and coping skills of birth parents who actively participate in adoption plans. Attention to the needs of birth parents in the months after the adoption has rarely been the practice of adoption workers, concentrating as they have done on 'settling in' the child with its adoptive parents. The case for help in this phase for birth mothers has been accepted and, if the reports of the men are in any way indicative of the feelings of other birth fathers, then support ought to be extended to birth fathers too. This relates to the final point in this chapter, concerning as it does the negative way in which birth fathers may be regarded and the attendant disadvantage to the child should this be the case.

A study of contemporary social work adoption case files has found an absence of information about birth fathers (*Family Studies*, Winter 1998). The case of the birth father who won custody of his two-year-old daughter after discovering that she had been placed in foster care (*Mail on Sunday*, 1 April 2001) also shows that adoption practitioners may not regard the birth father as a resource, or his position as significant for the child. Others may not necessarily agree with this latter point of the long-term significance of the birth father. *The Irish Times* has reported on a case where a couple who were in the step-parent adoption process wanted to re-register the birth in order that the current partner be shown as the biological father. Their attitude was that 'the natural father was out of the frame, the child had an effective father so what was the big deal?' (17 January 2001). Good adoption practice pre-placement would seem to require the gathering of the fullest possible information about the birth father and for the safeguarding of his significance – for the benefit of the child who may seek knowledge of him in later life. The children of birth parents are best served when birth fathers are placed in the same theoretical position as birth mothers, thus officially acknowledging to the child its reality of dual parentage.

The birth fathers in this study have talked of emotions normally associated with social fatherhood without ever having parented the child in question. This suggests that fatherhood is more complex than we have hither understood it to be. It is now the task of Government, researchers and professionals (all of us) to act on what we know rather than what we think we know about fathers in general and birth fathers in particular.

References

ADSS (Association of Directors of Social Services)-BAAF (British Agencies for Adoption and Fostering) (2000) 'What is adoption?' Joint Briefing. London: ADSS.

Ainsworth, M. (1969) 'Object relations, dependency and attachment: a theoretical overview of the infant-mother relationship'. *Child Development 40,* 969–1025.

Ainsworth, M. (1991) 'Attachments and other affectional bonds across the life cycle'. In C. Parkes, J. Stevenson-Hinde and P. Marris (eds) *Attachment Across the Life Cycle.* London and New York: Routledge.

Anglim, E. (1965) 'The adopted child's heritage – two natural parents'. *Child Welfare* June, 339–343.

Andry, R. (1962) 'Paternal and maternal roles and delinquency'. In *Deprivation of Maternal Care: A Reassessment of its Effects.* Public Health Papers 14. Geneva: World Health Organisation.

Argent, H. (ed) (1988) *Keeping the Doors Open: A Review of Post-adoption Services.* London: BAAF Practice Services No. 15.

Baran, A. and Pannor, R. (1990) 'Open adoption'. In D. Brodzinsky and M. Schechter (eds) *The Psychology of Adoption.* New York: Open University Press.

Baran, A., Pannor, R. and Sorosky, A. (1977) 'The lingering pain of surrendering a child'. *Psychology Today 88,* 58–60.

Barber, D. (1975) *Unmarried Fathers.* London: Hutchinson.

Beail, N. (1982) 'The role of the father during pregnancy and childbirth'. In N. Beail and J. McGuire (eds) *Fathers: Psychological Perspectives.* London: Junction Books.

Benedek, T. (1970) 'Fatherhood and providing'. In E. Anthony and T. Benedek (eds) *Parenthood.* Boston: Little, Brown.

Bell, I. (1943) *The Life of Johnny Reb: The Common Soldier of the Confederacy.* Lewisberry, Penn.: Charter Press.

Berg, S. and Wynne-Edwards, K. (2001) 'Changes in testosterone, cortisol and estradiol levels in men becoming fathers'. *Mayo Clinic Proceedings 76,* 582–592.

Berryman, S. (1997) 'Understanding reunion: reflections on research from the Post-Adoption Resource Centre, NSW'. In *The Sixth Australian Conference on Adoption*. Brisbane: Committee for Sixth Australian Conference on Adoption.

Blendis, J. (1982) 'Men's experiences of their own fathers'. In N. Beail and J. McGuire (eds) *Fathers: Psychological Perspectives*. London: Junction Books.

Blyth, E. (1999) 'Secrets and lies: barriers to the exchange of genetic origins information following donor assisted conception'. *Adoption and Fostering 23*, 49–58.

Bouchier, P., Lambert, L. and Triseliotis, J. (1991) *Parting with a Child for Adoption: The Mother's Perspective*. London: BAAF.

Bowlby, J. (1969) *Attachment and Loss. Vol. 1 Attachment*. London: Hogarth Press.

Bowlby, J. (1973) *Attachment and Loss. Vol. 2 Separation: Anxiety and Anger*. London: Hogarth Press.

Bowlby, J. (1979) *The Making and Breaking of Affectional Bonds*. London: Tavistock Publications.

Bowlby, J. (1980) *Attachment and Loss. Vol. 3 Loss: Sadness and Depression*. London: Hogarth Press.

Bowlby, J. (1984) 'Caring for the young: influences on development'. In R. Cohen, B. Cohler and S. Weissman (eds) *Parenthood: A Psychodynamic Perspective*. New York: The Guildford Press.

Bradshaw, J. and Miller, J. (1991) *Lone Parents in the UK. DSS Research Report No. 6*. London: HMSO.

Bradshaw, J., Skinner, C., Stimson, C. and Williams, J. (1999) *Absent Fathers?* London: Routledge.

Brearley, P., Hall, F., Gutridge, P., Jones, G. and Roberts, G. (1980) *Admission to Residential Care*. London and New York: Tavistock Press.

Bretherton, I. (1991) 'The roots and growing points of attachment theory'. In C. Parkes, J. Stevenson-Hinde and P. Marris (eds) *Attachment Across the Life Cycle*. London and New York: Routledge.

Brinich, P. (1990) 'Adoption from the inside out: a psychoanalytic perspective'. In D. Brodzinsky and M. Schechter (eds) *The Psychology of Adoption*. New York: Open University Press.

Brodzinsky, A. (1990) 'Surrendering an infant for adoption: the birth mother experience'. In D. Brodzinsky and M. Schechter (eds) *The Psychology of Adoption*. New York: Open University Press.

Buckley, H. (1998) 'Filtering out fathers: The guarded nature of social work in child protection.' *Irish Journal of Social Work Research 1*, 1, 29–42.

Burgess, A. (1997) *Fatherhood Reclaimed: The Making of the Modern Father.* UK: Vermilion.

Burgess, A. and Ruxton, S. (1996) *Men and Their Children: Proposals for Public Policy.* London: Institute for Public Policy Reseach.

Burghes, L., Clarke, L. and Cronin, N. (1997) *Fathers and Fatherhood in Britain.* London: Family Policy Studies Centre.

Byrd Dean, A. (1988) 'The case for confidential adoption'. *Public Welfare 37*, 3, 22–27.

Cabrera, N., Tamis-LeMonda, C., Bradley, R., Hofferth, S. and Lamb, M. (2000) 'Fatherhood in the twenty-first century'. *Child Development 71*, 1, 127–136.

Carsten, J. (2000) '"Knowing where you've come from": ruptures and continuities of time and kinship in narratives of adoption reunions'. *The Journal of the Royal Anthropological Institute 6*, 687–703.

Charlton, L., Crank, M., Kansara, K. and Oliver, C. (1998) *Still Screaming: Birth Parents Compulsorily Separated from their Children.* Manchester: After Adoption.

Chodorow, N. (1978) *The Reproduction of Mothering.* Berkeley: University of California Press.

Cicchini, M. (1993) *Development of Responsibility: The Experience of Birth Fathers in Adoption.* Perth, Western Australia: Adoption Research and Counselling Service.

Clapton, G. (1996a) writing as Colvin, G. 'A cache of feelings buried in a time capsule'. *The Scotsman*, 7 March 1996.

Clapton, G. (1996b) 'No more secrets and lies'. *Community Care*, 7 November 1996.

Clarke, S. and Popay, J. (1998) '"I'm just a bloke who's had kids": men and women on parenthood'. In J. Popay, J. Hearn and J. Edwards (eds) *Men, Gender Divisions and Welfare.* London: Routledge.

Cohen, T. (1993) 'What do fathers provide?: reconsidering the economic and nurturant dimensions of men as parents'. In J. Hood (ed) *Men, Work and Family.* Newbury Park, CA: Sage.

Cole, E. and Donley, K. (1990) 'History, values and placement policy issues in adoption'. In D. Brodzinsky and M. Schechter (eds) *The Psychology of Adoption.* New York: Open University Press.

Coleman, K. and Jenkins, E. (1998) *Elephants Never Forget.* UK: Signature Publications.

Coles, G. (1998) 'Being a birthfather'. In *Adoption Looking Back, Looking Forward*. New Zealand: Canterbury Adoption Awareness and Education Trust.

Coles, G. (2000) 'The unspoken burden'. In *The Seventh Australian Conference on Adoption*. Hobart: Committee for Seventh Australian Conference on Adoption.

Collier, R. (1995) *Masculinity, Law and the Family*. London and New York: Routledge.

Concerned United Birthparents *CUB Newsletter* January 1983.

Connolly, L. (1978) 'Boy fathers'. *Human Development 7*, 40–43.

Crowell, J. and Treboux, D. (1995) 'A review of adult attachment measures: implications for theory and research'. *Social Development 4*, 294–327.

Daniel, B. and Taylor, J. (1999) 'The rhetoric versus the reality: a critical perspective on practice with fathers in child care and child protection work'. *Child and Family Social Work 4*, 3, 209–220.

Daniels, C. (1998) Introduction in C. Daniels (ed) *Lost Fathers: The Politics of Fatherlessness in America*. Basingstoke and London: McMillan.

Daniels, P. and Weingarten, K. (1982) *Sooner or Later: The Timing of Parenthood in Adult Lives*. New York: Norton.

Davidoff, L., Doolittle, M., Fink, J. and Holden, K. (1999) *The Family Story: Blood, Contract and Intimacy, 1830–1960*. London and New York: Longman.

Department of Health (1993) *Adoption: The Future*. DoH: London.

Department of Health (1999) *Supporting Families: A Consultation Document*. London: HMSO.

Department of Health (2000a) *Adoption: A New Approach*.

Department of Health (2000b) *Draft National Adoption Standards for England, Scotland and Wales*. DoH: London.

Department of Health (2000c) *Intermediary Services for Birth Relatives: Practice Guidelines*. DoH: London.

Department of Health and Welsh Office (1992) *Review of Adoption Law. Report to Ministers of an Interdepartmental Working Group. A Consultation Document*. London: HMSO.

Departmental Commission on the Adoption of Children (1954) *Report*. London: HMSO.

Departmental Committee on Adoption of Children (1970) *Adoption of Children Working Paper*. London: HMSO.

Departmental Committee on the Adoption of Children (Houghton Report) (1972) *Report*. London: HMSO.

Deykin, E., Campbell, L. and Patti, P. (1984) 'The post-adoption experience of surrendering parents'. *American Journal of Orthopsychiatry 54*, 271–280.

Deykin, E., Patti, P. and Ryan, J. (1988) 'Fathers of adopted children: a study of the impact of child surrender on birth fathers'. *American Journal of Orthopsychiatry 58*, 240–248.

Diamond, M. (1995a) 'Becoming a father: a psychoanalytic perspective on the forgotten parent'. In J. Shapiro, M. Diamond and M. Greenberg (eds) *Becoming A Father: Contemporary Social, Developmental and Clinical Perspectives*. New York: Springer.

Diamond, M. (1995b) 'The emergence of the father as the watchful protector of the mother-infant dyad'. In J. Shapiro, M. Diamond and M. Greenberg (eds) *Becoming A Father: Contemporary Social, Developmental and Clinical Perspectives*. New York: Springer.

Dienhart, A. (1998) *Reshaping Fatherhood: The Social Construction of Shared Parenting*. Thousand Oaks, CA: Sage.

Doherty, W. (1997) 'The best of times and the worst of times: fathering as a contested arena of academic discourse'. In A. Hawkins and D. Dollahite (eds) *Generative Fathering: Beyond Deficit Perspectives*. Thousand Oaks, CA: Sage.

Edinburgh Family Service Unit (2001) *Dad's The Word*. Edinburgh: FSU.

Edwards, J. (1998) 'Screening out men: or "Has Mum changed her washing powder recently?"' In J. Popay, J. Hearn and J. Edwards (eds) *Men, Gender Divisions and Welfare*. London: Routledge.

Edwards, C. and Williams, C. (2000) 'Adopting change: birth mothers in maternity homes today'. *Gender and Society 14*, 160–183.

Eggebeen, D. and Knoester, C. (2001) 'Does fatherhood matter for men?' *Journal of Marriage and the Family 63*, 2, 381–393.

Fahlberg, V. (1991) *A Child's Journey Through Placement*. London: BAAF.

Family Policy Unit (1998) *Boys, Young Men and Fathers: A Ministerial Seminar*. London: Home Office.

Family Studies (1998) Newsletter of the *Contact after Adoption* and the *Growing up in Foster Care* studies. Number 2. Winter. School of Social Work University of East Anglia, Norwich.

Farrar, T. (1997) '"What we did to those poor girls!" – the hospital culture that promoted adoption'. In *The Sixth Australian Conference on Adoption*. Brisbane: Committee for Sixth Australian Conference on Adoption.

Feast, J. (1994) *Preparing for Reunion*. London: The Children's Society.

Feast, J., Marwood, M., Seabrook, S. and Webb, E. (1998) *Preparing for Reunion* (new edition). London: The Children's Society.

Feast, J. 'Mother and child reunion'. *Community Care*, 27 August 1998.

Feast, J. and Smith, J. (1993) 'Working on behalf of birth families – The Children's Society experience'. *Adoption and Fostering 7*, 33–40.

Federal Interagency Forum on Children and Family Statistics (1998) *Nurturing Fatherhood: Improving Data and Research on Male Fertility, Family Formation and Fatherhood.* Washington, USA: Child Trends Inc.

Field, J. (1991) 'Views of New Zealand birth mothers on search and reunion'. In A. Mullender (ed) *Open Adoption: The Philosophy and the Practice.* London: BAAF.

Finch, J. and Mason, J. (1990) 'Divorce, remarriage and family obligations'. *Sociological Review 38*, 219–246.

Finch, J. and Mason, J. (1991) 'Obligations of kinship in contemporary Britain: is there normative agreement?' *British Journal of Sociology 32*, 3, 345–367.

Flouri, E. and Buchanan, A. 'Father Time'. *Community Care*, 10 October 2001.

Forna, A. (1998) *Mother of All Myths: How Society Moulds and Constrains Mothers.* London: HarperCollins.

Freeley, M. 'He's 14, his girlfriend is pregnant, and he'll be a great dad'. *The Guardian*, 8 September 1999.

Furstenberg, F. and Cherlin, A. (1991) *Divided Families: What Happens to Children when Parents Part.* London: Harvard.

Furstenberg, F., Nord, C., Peterson, J. and Zill, N. (1983) 'The life course of children of divorce: marital disruption and parental conflict'. *American Sociological Review 48*, 656–668.

General Register Office (1999) Annual Report 1997 Section 9: Adoptions and Re-registrations.

Ghate, D., Shaw, C. and Hazel, N. (2000) *Engaging Fathers in Preventative Services: Fathers and Family Centres.* York: Joseph Rowntree Foundation and York YPS.

Gould, P. (1995) 'In response to "Reunions between adoptees and birth parents"'. Letter to *Social Work 40*, 288.

Greenberg, M. (1985) *The Birth of a Father.* New York: Continuum.

Greif, G. and Bailey, C. (1990) 'Where are the fathers in social work literature?' *Families in Society 71*, 88–92.

Grey, E. (1971) *A Survey of Adoption in Great Britain.* Home Office Research Unit and Social Survey Division of Office of Population Censuses and Surveys. London: HMSO.

Griswold, R. (1998) 'The history and politics of fatherlessness'. In C. Daniels (ed) *Lost Fathers: The Politics of Fatherlessness in America*. Basingstoke and London: McMillan.

Gurwitt, A. (1995) 'Aspects of prospective fatherhood'. In J. Shapiro, M. Diamond and M. Greenberg (eds) *Becoming A Father: Contemporary Social, Developmental and Clinical Perspectives*. New York: Springer.

Harper, J. (1993) 'What does she look like? What children want to know about their birth parents'. *Adoption and Fostering 17*, 27–29.

Hawkins, A., Christiansen, S., Sargent, K. and Hill, E. (1995) 'Rethinking father's involvement in child care: a developmental perspective'. In W. Marsiglio (ed) *Fatherhood: Contemporary Theory, Research and Social Policy*. Thousand Oaks: Sage.

Hill, D. (1998) *The Guardian*, 2 December 1998.

Hilpern, K. 'Founding fathers'. *The Times Magazine*, 4 July 1998, 76–80.

Hirst, J. (1999) 'Putting the Children First'. *Community Care*, 22–24.

Howe, D. (1990) 'The Post-Adoption Centre: the first three years'. *Adoption and Fostering 4*, 27–31.

Howe, D. (1995) *Attachment Theory for Social Work Practice*. Basingstoke and London: McMillan.

Howe, D., Sawbridge, P. and Hinings, D. (1992) *Half a Million Women: Mothers who Lose their Children by Adoption*. London: Penguin.

Howe, D. and Feast, J. (2000) *Adoption, Search and Reunion: The Long Term Experience of Adopted Adults*. London: The Children's Society.

Hughes, B. (1996) 'Birth mothers and their mental health: uncharted territory'. *British Journal of Social Work 26*, 609–625.

Hughes, B. and Logan, J. (1993) *Birth Parents: The Hidden Dimension*. University of Manchester.

Inglis, K. (1984) *Living Mistakes: Mothers Who Consented to Adoption*. Sydney: Allen and Unwin.

Iredale, S. (1997) *Reunions: True Stories of Adoptees' Meetings with their Natural Parents*. London: HMSO.

Johnson, M. (1988) *Strong Mothers, Weak Wives: The Search For Gender Equality*. Berkeley: University of California Press.

Katz, A. (1999) *Leading Lads*. East Molesey, Surrey: Young Voice.

Kalmuss, D., Namerow, P. and Cushman, L. (1991) 'Adoption versus parenting among young pregnant women'. *Family Planning Perspectives 23*, 17–23.

Kraemer, S. quoted in 'Fatherhood at Crisis Point' 21 April *The Observer*, 1 October 1996.

Krampe, E. and Fairweather, P. (1993) 'Father presence and family formation: a theoretical reformulation'. *Journal of Family Issues 14*, 573–593.

La Rossa, R. (1986) *Becoming a Parent.* Newbury Park, CA: Sage.

Lamb, M. (1981) *The Role of the Father in Child Development.* New York: Wiley.

Lamb, M. (1987) Preface in M. Lamb (ed) *The Father's Role: Cross-Cultural Perspectives.* New Jersey: Lawrence Erlbuam Associates.

Lamb, M. (1996) *What are Fathers for? Presentation at Men and Their Children Conference.* London: Institute for Public Policy Research.

Lewis, C. (1982) '"A feeling you can't scratch?": the effect of pregnancy and birth on married men'. In N. Beail and J. McGuire (eds) *Fathers: Psychological Perspectives.* London: Junction Books.

Lewis, C. (1986) *Becoming a Father.* Milton Keynes: Open University Press.

Lewis, C. (1994) 'Changing fatherhood? A European perspective'. *Children In Scotland.* Special Issue Newsletter No. 8, September 1994.

Lewis, C. (1995) 'What opportunities are open to fathers?' In P. Moss (ed) *Father Figures in the Families of the 1990s.* Edinburgh: Children in Scotland/HMSO.

Lewis, C. (2000) 'A man's place is in the home: fathers and families in the UK'. London: Joseph Rowntree Foundation/YPS.

Lewis, C. and O'Brien, M. (1987) *Reassessing Fatherhood.* London: Sage.

Lightman, E. and Schlesinger, B. (1982) 'Pregnant adolescents in maternity homes: some professional concerns'. In I. Stuart, I. and C. Wells (eds) *Pregnancy in Adolescence: Needs, Problems and Management.* New York: Van Nostrand Reinhold Company.

Logan, J. (1996) 'Birth mothers and their mental health: uncharted territory'. *British Journal of Social Work 26*, 609–625.

Lupton, D. and Barclay, L. (1997) *Constructing Fatherhood: Discourses and Experiences.* Thousand Oaks, CA: Sage.

Mackey, W. (1985) *Fathering Behaviours: The Dynamics of the Man-Child Bond.* New York and London: Plenum Press.

Mackey, W. (2001) 'Support for the existence of an independent man-to-child affiliative bond: fatherhood as a biocultural invention'. *Psychology of Men and Masculinity 2*,1, 51–66.

Mander, R. (1995) *The Care of a Mother Grieving a Baby Relinquished for Adoption.* Aldershot: Avebury.

March, K. (1995) *The Stranger Who Bore Me: Adoptee-Birth Mother Relationships.* Toronto: University of Toronto Press.

Marsiglio, W. (1995a) 'Fatherhood scholarship: an overview and agenda for the future'. In W. Marsiglio (ed) *Fatherhood: Contemporary Theory, Research and Social Policy.* Thousand Oaks, CA: Sage.

Marsiglio, W. (1995b) 'Fathers' diverse life course patterns and roles: theory and social interventions'. In W. Marsiglio (ed) *Fatherhood: Contemporary Theory, Research and Social Policy.* Thousand Oaks, CA: Sage.

Marsiglio, W., Amato, P., Day, R. and Lamb, M. (2000) 'Scholarship on fatherhood in the 1990s and beyond'. *Journal of Marriage and the Family 62*, 4, 1173–1191.

Mason, M. (1995) *Out of the Shadows: Birthfathers' Stories.* Edina, Minnesota: O.J. Howard Publishing.

Masson, J., Harrison, C. and Pavlovic, A. (1997) 'Working with children and "lost parents"'. Findings. *Social Care Research 98*, October.

May, K. (1982) 'Factors contributing to first-time fathers' readiness for fatherhood: an exploratory study'. *Family Relations 31*, 353–361.

May, K. (1995) 'Men and high-risk childbearing'. In J. Shapiro, M. Diamond and M. Greenberg (eds) *Becoming A Father: Contemporary Social, Developmental and Clinical Perspectives.* New York: Springer.

McCroy, R. (1991) 'American experience and research on openness'. *Adoption and Fostering 15*, 99–110. London: BAAF.

McHaffie, H. and Fowlie, P. (1996) *Life, Death and Decisions.* Cheshire, England: Hochland and Hochland.

McKee, L. and O'Brien, M. (1982a) 'The desire to father: reproductive ideologies and involuntarily childless men'. In L. McKee and M. O'Brien (eds) *The Father Figure.* London: Tavistock Publications.

McKee, L. and O'Brien, M. (1982b) '"The father figure": some current orientations and historical perspectives'. In L. McKee and M. O'Brien (eds) *The Father Figure.* London: Tavistock Publications.

McMillan, R. and Irving, G. (1997) *Heart of Reunion: Some Experiences of Reunion in Scotland.* Ilford: Barnardo's.

McWhinnie, A. (1994) 'The concept of "open adoption" – how valid is it?' In A. McWhinnie and J. Smith (eds) *Current Human Dilemmas in Adoption. The Challenge for Parents, Practitioners and Policy-Makers.* University of Dundee.

Mead, M. (1962) 'A cultural anthropologist's approach to maternal deprivation delinquency'. In *Deprivation of Maternal Care: A Reassessment of its Effects. Public Health Papers 14.* Geneva: World Health Organisation.

Menard, B. (1997) 'A birth father and adoption in the perinatal setting'. *Social Work and Health Care 24*, No. 3/4 153–163.

Mercer, R., Ferketich, S., De Joseph, J., May, K. and Sollid, D. (1988) 'Further exploration of maternal and paternal foetal attachment'. *Research in Nursing and Health 11*, 2, 83–95.

Millen, L. and Roll, S. (1985) 'Solomon's mothers: a special case of pathological bereavement'. *The American Journal of Orthopsychiatry 53*, 411– 418.

Milligan, C. and Dowie, A. (1998) *What Do Children Need From Their Fathers?* Edinburgh: Centre for Theology and Public Issues, University of Edinburgh.

Modell, J. (1986) 'In search: the purported biological basis of parenthood'. *American Ethnologist 13*, 646–661.

Modell, J. (1994) *Kinship with Strangers: Adoptions and Interpretations of Kinship in American Culture.* Berkley: University of California Press.

Morrison, B. (1998) *'And When Did You Last See Your Father?'* London: Granta.

Motluk, A. (2000) 'Father instinct.' *Orgyn XI 4*, 24–27.

Mullender, A. and Kearn, S. (1997) *'I'm Here Waiting': Birth Relatives' Views on Part II of the Adoption Contact Register for England and Wales.* London: BAAF.

National Association for Mental Health, (1960) *A Survey Based on Adoption Case Records.* London.

Natural Parents Support Group (1993) *Newsletter* Spring, 1993.

NORCAP (1998) 'Charlie'. *Norcap News 53*, Spring.

Owens, D. (1982) 'The desire to father: reproductive ideologies and involuntary childless men'. In L. McKee and M. O'Brien (eds) *The Father Figure.* London: Tavistock Publications.

Pacheo, F. and Eme, R. (1993) 'An outcome study of the reunion between adoptees and biological parents'. *Child Welfare 72*, 53–64.

Pannor, R., Baran, A. and Sorosky, A. (1978) 'Birth parents who relinquished babies for adoption revisited'. *Family Process 17*, 329–337.

Pannor, R., Massarik, F. and Evans, B. (1971) *The Unmarried Father.* New York: Springer.

Parkes, C. (1972) *Bereavement: Studies of Grief in Adult Life.* Harmondsworth: Penguin.

Pasley, K. and Minton, C. (1997) 'Generative fathering after divorce and remarriage: beyond the "disappearing dad"'. In A. Hawkins and D. Dollahite (eds) *Generative Fathering: Beyond Deficit Perspectives.* Thousand Oaks, CA: Sage.

Petrie, A. (1998) *Gone to an Aunt's: Remembering Canada's Homes for Unwed Mothers.* Toronto: McClelland and Stewart.

Performance and Innovation Unit (2000) *Adoption: Prime Minister's Review.* Crown Office.

Pickford, R. (1992) 'Promoting natural links – recent cases on adoption'. *Journal of Child Law* June, 138–140.

Pickford, R. (1999) 'Fathers, marriage and the law'. London: Family Policy Studies Centre.

Pill, C. J. (1990) 'Stepfamilies: Redefining the Family'. *Family Relations 39,* 186–193.

Platts, H. (1968) 'A public adoption agency's approach to natural fathers'. *Child Welfare* Vol. XLVII, 530–553.

Pleck, J. (1995) 'The father wound: implications for expectant fathers'. In J. Shapiro, M. Diamond and M. Greenberg (eds) *Becoming A Father: Contemporary Social, Developmental and Clinical Perspectives.* New York: Springer.

Post-Adoption Social Workers Group (1987) *Meetings – A New Beginning. Experiences of Reunion after Adoption.* Postal Bag 1, Paddington NSW, Australia.

Powell, S. and Warren, J. (1997) *The Easy Way Out? Birth Mothers of Adopted Children – The Hidden Side of Adoption.* London: Minerva.

The Princes Trust (2001) *Yes You Can: The Views and Hopes of Disadvantaged Young People.* London: The Crown Office.

Raynor, L. (1971) *Giving Up A Baby For Adoption.* London: Association of British Adoption Agencies.

Rich, A. (1995 re-issue) *Of Woman Born.* New York: W.W. Norton.

Richards, M. (1982) 'How should we approach the study of fathers?' In L. McKee and M. O'Brien (eds) *The Father Figure.* London: Tavistock Publications.

Richman, J. (1982) 'Men's experiences of pregnancy and childbirth'. In L. McKee and M. O'Brien (eds) *The Father Figure.* London: Tavistock Publications.

Rockel, J. and Ryburn, M. (1988) *Adoption Today: Change and Choice in New Zealand.* Auckland: Heineman Reid.

Roll, S., Millen, L. and Backland, B. (1986) 'Solomon's mothers: mourning mothers who relinquish their children for adoption'. In T. Rando (ed) *Parental Loss of a Child.* Illinois: Research Press Co.

Rolphe, J. (1999) *'Young, Unemployed, Unmarried… Fathers Talking'.* London: Working With Men.

Roopnarine, J. and Miller, B. (1985) 'Transitions to fatherhood'. In S. Hanson and F. Bozett (eds) *Dimensions of Fatherhood.* New York: Sage.

Rosenberg, E. (1992) *The Adoption Life Cycle.* New York: The Free Press.

Ross, J. (1982) 'The roots of fatherhood: excursions into a lost literature'. In S. Cath, A. Gurwitt and J. Ross (eds) *Father and Child: Developmental and Clinical Perspectives.* Boston: Little, Brown.

Rossi, A. (1977) 'A bio-social perspective on parenting'. *Daedalus 87*, 1–31.

Rowe, J. (1977) 'The reality of the adoptive family'. In *Child Adoption: A Selection of Articles on Adoption Theory and Practice.* London: BAAF.

Rutter, M. (1972) *Maternal Deprivation Reassessed.* Harmondsworth: Penguin.

Rutter, M. (1995) 'Clinical implications of attachment concepts: retrospect and prospect'. *Journal of Child Psychology and Psychiatry 36*, 549–571.

Ryan, M. (1996) 'Families of origin'. In J. Tunnard (ed) *Adoption and Birth Families: Getting Law and Practice Right for Their Children.* London: Family Rights Group.

Ryan, M. (2000) *Working With Fathers.* Oxon: Radcliffe Medical Press.

Ryburn, M. (1996) 'Secrecy and openness: a historical perspective'. In J. Tunnard (ed) *Adoption and Birth Families: Getting Law and Practice Right for Their Children.* London: Family Rights Group.

Sachdev, P. (1991) 'The birth father. A neglected element in the adoption equation'. *Families in Society*, Human Services 72, 131–138.

Sachdev, P. (1992) 'Adoption reunion and after: a study of the search process and experience of adoptees'. *Child Welfare LXXI*, 53–68.

Sarre, S. (1996) *A Place for Fathers: Fathers and Social Policy in the Post-War Period.* London: International Centre for Economics and Related Disciplines, London School of Economics.

Sawbridge, P. (1980) 'Seeking new parents: a decade of development'. In J. Triseliotis (ed) *New Developments in Foster Care and Adoption.* London: Routledge and Kegan Paul.

Sawbridge, P. (1991) 'On behalf of birth parents'. In A. Mullender (ed) *Open Adoption: The Philosophy and the Practice.* London: BAAF.

Scarman, Mr. Justice, (1968) 'Legal Rights – Session 1'. In *The Human Rights of Those Born Out of Wedlock.* London: National Council for the Unmarried Mother and Her Child.

Schechter, M. and Bertocci, D. (1990) 'The meaning of the search'. In D. Brodzinsky and M. Schechter (eds) *The Psychology of Adoption.* New York: Open University Press.

Schwartz, L. (1986) 'Unwed fathers and adoption custody disputes'. *American Journal of Family Therapy 14*, 4, 347–355.

Scottish Office (1993) *The Future of Adoption Law in Scotland: A Consultation Paper.* Social Work Services Group: Scotland.

Seel, R. (1987) *The Uncertain Father: Exploring Modern Fatherhood.* Bath: Gateway Publications.

Shapiro, J., Diamond, M. and Greenberg, M. (1995) *Becoming a Father: Contemporary Social, Developmental and Clinical Perspectives.* New York: Springer.

Shaw, M. and Hill, M. (1998) Introduction. In M. Hill and M. Shaw (eds) *Signposts in Adoption: Policy, Practice and Research Issues.* London: BAAF.

Shawyer, J. (1979) *Death By Adoption.* Auckland: Cicada Press.

Silber, K. and Speedlin, P. (1983) *Dear Birth Mother.* Texas: Corona.

Simpson, B., McCarthy, P. and Walker, J. (1995) *Being There: Fathers After Divorce.* Newcastle upon Tyne: Relate Centre for Family Studies.

Singh, D. and Newburn, M. (2000) *Becoming A Father.* Glasgow: NCT.

Sorosky, A., Baran, A. and Pannor, R. (1974) 'The reunions of adoptees and birth relatives'. *Journal of Youth and Adolescence 3*, 195–206.

Sorosky, A., Baran, A. and Pannor, R. (1978) *The Adoption Triangle.* New York: Anchor Doubleday.

Speak, S. (2001) 'Young single fathers – problems or possibilities?' *Young People's Health Network.* Health Development Agency 15, Summer, 2–3.

Speak, S., Cameron, S. and Gilroy, R. (1997) *Young Single Fathers: Participation in Fatherhood – Barriers and Bridges.* London: Family Policy Studies Centre.

Speirs, J. and Paterson, L. (1994) 'Dilemmas for birth parents in contact and openness'. In A. McWhinnie and J. Smith. (eds) *Current Human Dilemmas in Adoption: The Challenge for Parents Practitioners and Policy-Makers.* University of Dundee.

Tabak, S. (1990) *Self Search. A Program For Adult Adopted Persons.* Australia: Community Services Victoria.

Tanfer, K. and Mott, F. (1998) 'The meaning of fatherhood for men'. In *Nurturing Fatherhood: Improving Data and Research on Male Fertility, Family Formation and Fatherhood.* Federal Interagency Forum on Children and Family Statistics Washington: Child Trends Inc.

Thoburn, J. (1992) *Appendix C in Review of Adoption Law: Report to Ministers of an Interdepartmental Working Group. A Consultation Document.* October 1992. London: Department of Health and Welsh Office.

Trinder, L. (2000) 'The rights and wrongs of post-adoption intermediary services for birth relatives.' *Adoption and Fostering 24*, 19–25.

Triseliotis, J. (1970) *Evaluation of Adoption Policy and Practice.* Edinburgh: University of Edinburgh.

Triseliotis, J. (1973) *In Search of Origins: The Experiences of Adopted People.* London: Routledge and Kegan Paul.

Triseliotis, J. (1977) 'Identity and adoption'. In *Child Adoption: A Selection of Articles on Adoption Theory and Practice.* London: BAAF.

Triseliotis, J. (1991) (ed) *Adoption Services in Scotland: Recent Research Findings and their Implications.* Edinburgh: Scottish Office Central Research Unit Papers.

Trotter, J. (1997) 'The failure of social work researchers, teachers and practitioners to acknowledge or engage non-abusing fathers: a preliminary discussion'. *Social Work Education 16,* 63–76.

Tugendhat, J. (1992) *The Adoption Triangle.* London: Bloomsbury.

Turner, B. and Rennell, T. (1995) *When Daddy came Home: How Family Life Changed Forever in 1945.* London: Hutchinson.

Wadia-Ells, S. (1996) (ed) *The Adoption Reader: Birth Mothers, Adoptive Mothers and Adopted Daughters Tell Their Stories.* London: The Women's Press.

Warin, J., Soloman, Y., Lewis, C. and Langford, W. (1999) *Fathers, Work and Family Life.* London: Family Policy Studies Centre.

Watson, K. (1986) 'Birth families: living with the adoption decision'. *Public Welfare,* Spring, 5–10.

Weinreb, M. and Murphy, C. (1988) 'The birth mother: a feminist perspective for the helping professional'. *Women and Therapy 7,* 23–26.

Weiss, R. (1991) 'The attachment bond in childhood and adulthood'. In C. Parkes, J. Stevenson-Hinde and P. Marris (eds) *Attachment Across the Life Cycle.* London and New York: Routledge.

Wells, S. (1993a) 'Post-traumatic stress in birth mothers'. *Adoption and Fostering 17,* 30–32.

Wells, S. (1993b) 'What do birth mothers want?' *Adoption and Fostering 17,* 22–26.

Wells, S. (1994) *Within Me, Without Me: Adoption, an Open and Shut Case?* London: Scarlet Press.

Williams, F. (1998) 'Troubled masculinities in social policy discourses: fatherhood'. In J. Popay, J. Hearn and J. Edwards (eds) *Men, Gender Divisions and Welfare.* London: Routledge.

Williams, R. and Robertson, S. (1999) 'Fathers and health visitors: "a secret agent thing"'. *Community Practitioner 72,* March.

Willmott, P. (1977) 'For fathers as for mothers'. *Social Work Today 8,* 19 April.

Winkler, R. and van Keppel, M. (1984) *Relinquishing Mothers in Adoption: Their Long-term Adjustment (Monograph No. 3).* Melbourne: Institute of Family Studies.

Wilson, E. (1977) *Women and the Welfare State.* London: Tavistock.

Wolson, P. (1995) 'Some reflections on adaptive grandiosity in fatherhood'. In J. Shapiro, M. Diamond and M. Greenberg (eds) *Becoming A Father: Contemporary Social, Developmental and Clinical Perspectives.* New York: Springer.

Yow, V. (1994) *Recording Oral History: A Practical Guide for Social Scientists.* Thousand Oaks, CA: Sage.

Subject Index

abdication of responsibility
  birth fathers 39–41, 203
  birth fathers: research sample
    73, 76, 83
absent fathers 50, 53
adopted children
  attitudes to birth fathers 37–8
  desire to search for birth
    parents 38, 39, 63
adoption 55, 63, 75–6, 77,
  210–12
  and birth fathers 33, 35, 37,
    89
  and birth fathers: research
    sample 78, 89–113
  and birth mothers 36, 37, 91,
    208
  and birth parents access to
    information on 166–9
  consent to 98–9, 101, 102,
    103, 104–5, 109
  effects of 33, 35, 36, 145–8
  emotional responses to
    105–13, 115–24, 116,
    125–41, 130
  government policies 17–27,
    207–10
  intervention by parents of birth
    parents 90–1, 92
  negative effects of 107–8
  participation and choices in 94,
    110–11, 111
  proceedings 93–101, 94–6,
    104–5, 207–10
  reactions to 89–93, 96–101,
    101, 201
  reasons for 90–2

and social workers 114–15
societal attitudes to 22, 113
statistics 17–20, 18, 19
and welfare workers 114–15
Adoption Contact Registers (ACR)
  43–6, 65, 156, 198, 209–10
  statistics 44–5
adoptive parents 22, 32, 37, 175
Association of Directors of Social
  Work and British Agencies
  for Adoption 208
attachment
  and birth fathers: research
    sample 183–7

bereavement see loss and
  bereavement
'birth father'
  and 'birth parent' terminology
    42
birth fathers see also birth fathers:
  research sample
  abdication of responsibility
    39–41, 203
  and adoption 33, 35, 37, 89
  and caring 59
  desire to recover adopted child
    34, 36
  desire to search for adopted
    child 33–5, 64
  legal rights 40
  negative stereotyping of
    49–51, 53, 201, 203
  numbers 43–6
  parenting roles 29–32, 31
  professionals' attitudes to
    39–43, 203–6, 207
  research into 20–7, 29–46,
    63–87
  and self–esteem 36
  as sperm donors 47, 51, 207
  status of 24–7, 41

birth fathers: research sample
 abdication of responsibility 73,
  76, 83
 and adoption 78, 89–113
  consent to 98–9, 101, 102,
   103, 104–5, 109
  emotional responses 105–13,
   115–24, 125–41, 130
  negative effects 107–8
  opposition to 96–8, 100,
   101, 102, 103, 104,
   109–10, 201
  participation and choices in
   94, 110–11, 111
  proceedings 94–6, 104–5
  reactions to 96–101, 101,
   201
 ages at births of children 66
 and attachment 183–7
 birth years of children 76
 and births 77–87
 and caring 76, 122, 157, 173
 case profiles 80, 90, 163
 and child contact 79–82,
  155–87
 and curiosity 131, 159
 desire to search for adopted
  child 155–66, 158, 178,
  201
 and expiation 160–1
 and fatherhood 71–4, 77–83,
  85, 86–7, 101, 103, 104,
  111–13, 126, 191–9
 and grief 117–20, 129, 206
 and guilt 137–8
 identification problems 64
 interviews with 66–7
 and parenthood 133–4
 and powerlessness 120–1, 130
 and pregnancy 67–76, 83–7
 professionals' attitudes to 79,
  80, 81, 113, 114–15

 qualification for inclusion 63
 and regret 136–7
 relationships with adoptive
  parents 175–9
 relationships with birth
  mothers 68, 79, 138–45
 relationships with other
  partners 145–8
 responses to societal changes
  66–7, 95
 and responsibility 132–3
 and 'restitution of self' 161–4
 and self–esteem 116, 174
 and sense of loss 85–6, 135–6,
  152–3, 197–8, 201
 and separation 101–5
 support groups 169
 and worry 131–2
'birth mother'
 and 'birth parent' terminology
  41–3
birth mothers 34
 and adoption 36, 37, 91, 208
 emotional responses 116
 desire to search for adopted
  child 33–4, 160
 and motherhood 73–4
 numbers 18, 19, 19, 43–6
 and pregnancy 70
 professionals' attitudes to 40,
  114–15
 research into 20–7, 40
 self–esteem 36
 status of 23–4, 26, 41
'birth parent'
 and 'birth father' terminology
  42
 and 'birth mother' terminology
  41–3
birth parents see birth fathers; birth
  mothers

Child Support Act (1991) 51
Children's Act (1975) 63
Children's Act (1989) 51, 63
Concerned United Birthparents 33, 177
curiosity 131, 159

fatherhood 47–60, 97, 99, 101, 111–13, 115, 122–4, 191–9, 201, 212
 and birth fathers: research sample 71–4, 77–83, 85, 86–7, 101, 103, 104, 111–13, 126, 191–9
 and birth fathers' perceptions of 192
 and blood relationships 193–4
 and bonding 193, 202
 and caring 58, 192
 and childhood experiences of being parented 196–8
 history of 48–9
 and hormonal changes 195
 legal definitions 51–2
 and loss 85–6, 135–6, 152–3, 197–8, 201
 modern perceptions of 49–53
 negative stereotyping of 49–51, 53, 201
 and pregnancy 55–8, 71–4
 and psycho–biological factors 194–6
 research into 52, 53–8, 191–9
 societal definitions 47–8, 95
Fathers Direct 206

government adoption policies 17–27, 207–10
grief 117–20, 129, 206
guilt 137–8

illegitimate births
 societal attitudes to 22–3

Law Commission Report on Illegitimacy (1979) 51
loss and bereavement 85–6, 135–6, 152–3, 197–8, 201

maternity *see* motherhood
motherhood 58–60, 73–4, 126

National Childbirth Trust 202–3
National Family and Parenting Institute 203
National Fatherhood Initiative 206
Natural Parents Network 156
NORCAP 43

parenthood 133–4, 148–50
 birth fathers: research sample 133–4
parents of birth parents
 intervention in adoption 90–1, 92, 113–14
paternity see fatherhood
paternity leave 203
powerlessness of birth fathers 120–1, 130
pregnancy
 and birth fathers: research sample 67–76, 83–7
 and birth mothers 70
 and fatherhood 55–8, 71–4
professionals' attitudes
 to birth fathers 39–43, 203–6, 207
 to birth fathers: research sample 79, 80, 81, 113, 114–15
 to birth mothers 40, 114–15

regret 136–7
responsibility 132–3

self–esteem
    birth fathers 36
    birth fathers: research sample
       116, 174
    birth mothers 36
Short, Clare 45
social workers
    and adoption 114–15
sperm donation 47, 51, 207
status
    birth fathers 24–7, 41
    birth mothers 23–4, 26, 41
stereotyping
    birth fathers 49–51, 53, 201,
       203
    fatherhood 49–51, 53, 201

terminology
    'birth parent' and 'birth father'
      42

welfare workers
    and adoption 114–15
worry 131–2

Author Index

Ainsworth, Mary 183, 184,
  18–56, 195
Amato, P. 49, 54
Andry, R. 197
Anglim, E. 25, 94, 207, 209
Argent, 37

Backland, B. 136
Bailey, C. 203
Baran, A. 23, 24, 25, 39, 42, 126,
  135, 136
Barber, D. 54, 82, 197
Barclay, L. 48, 59, 133
Beail, N. 55
Bell, I. 193
Benedek, T. 57
Berg, S. 195
Berryman, S. 162
Bertocci, D. 25
Blendis, J. 48, 197
Blyth, E. 47
Bouchier, P. 20, 22, 23, 30, 68,
  77, 91, 116, 117, 137, 153,
  159, 168
Bowlby, John 183, 184
Bradley, R. 48
Bradshaw, J. 26, 49, 50, 51, 52,
  53, 205
Brearley, P. 120
Bretherton, I. 183
Brinich, P. 29, 30, 33, 60, 117,
  187
Brodzinsky, A. 20, 40, 41, 42, 58,
  117, 135n
Buchanan, A. 203
Buckley, 202

Burgess, A. 26, 48, 49, 50, 53, 54,
  55, 59, 60
Burghes, L. 23, 25, 47, 48, 49, 51,
  52, 59, 67, 95
Byrd Dean, A. 186

Cabrera, N. 48
Cameron, S. 49, 50, 59, 192
Campbell, L. 20, 34, 42, 147,
  162, 163, 195
Carsten, J. 208
Cherlin, A. 50
Chodorow, N. 73
Christiansen, S. 57, 58
Cicchini, M. 32, 34–6, 66, 89,
  105, 115, 116, 117, 120,
  129, 132, 161
Clapton, G. 17, 19, 37
Clarke, L. 23, 25, 47, 48, 49, 51,
  52, 59, 67, 95
Clarke, S. 53, 59
Cohen, T. 48, 194
Cole, E. 25
Coleman, K. 37, 156–7
Coles, G. 37
Collier, R. 52
Concerned United Birthparents 37,
  144, 177
Connolly, L. 23, 25, 82
Cronin, N. 23, 25, 47, 48, 49, 51,
  52, 59, 67, 95
Crowell, J. 184
Cushman, L. 65

Daniel, B. 41, 204, 207
Daniel, P. 55
Daniels, C. 52
Davidoff, L. 21, 22, 24, 48
Day, R. 49, 54
De Joseph, J. 58

Department of Health 17, 21, 43, 49, 167, 209
Departmental Committee on the Adoption of Children 55
Deykin, E. 20, 25, 32–3, 34, 39, 42, 96, 147, 162, 163, 166, 195
Diamond, M. 53, 55, 56, 57, 194
Dienhart, A. 48, 49, 55, 59
Doherty, W. 25, 48
Donley, K. 25
Doolittle, M. 21, 22, 24, 48

Edinburgh Family Service Unit 50
Edwards, C. 22, 65
Edwards, J. 49, 53, 204
Eggebeen, D. 52
Eliot, George 179n
Eme, R. 39
Engels, Matthew 58
Evans, B. 37, 73, 82, 84, 151, 197, 207

Fahlberg, V. 184, 185, 207
Fairweather, P. 56, 194–5
Family Policy Unit 50
Farrar, T. 22, 23
Feast, J. 12, 33–4, 37, 38, 167, 178, 181, 186, 208
Federal Interagency Forum on Children and Family Statistics 55
Ferketich, S. 58
Field, J. 166, 167
Finch, J. 176, 179
Fink, J. 21, 22, 24, 48
Flouri, E. 203
Forna, A. 73, 86
Fowlie, P. 120
Freeley, M. 53
Furstenberg, F. 50

Ghate, 202
Gilroy, R. 49, 50, 59, 192
Gould, P. 33
Greenberg, M. 53, 55
Grey, E. 18, 23
Grieff, G. 203
Griswold, R. 49
Gurwitt, A. 55
Gutridge, P. 120

Hall, F. 120
Harper, J. 31, 41
Harrison, C. 204
Hawkins, A. 57, 58
Hill, D. 50
Hill, E. 57, 58
Hill, M. 24
Hilpern, K. 37
Hinings, D. 17–18, 19, 20, 21, 23, 69, 73, 126, 133, 149, 161
Hirst, J. 17
Hofferth, S. 48
Holden, K. 21, 22, 24, 48
Howe, D. 17–18, 19, 20, 21, 23, 33–4, 43, 69, 73, 126, 133, 149, 161, 178, 181, 183, 185, 208
Howie, A. 50
Hughes, B. 20, 42, 43, 68, 76, 126, 132, 133, 137, 138, 141, 152, 162

Inglis, K. 68, 70, 135
Iredale, S. 181
Irving, G. 181

Jenkins, E. 37, 156–7
Johnson, M. 58
Jones, G. 120

Kalmuss, D. 65
Katz, A. 197
Kearn, S. 22, 34, 37, 43, 44, 45, 155, 166, 167, 169, 181, 191
Knoester, C. 52
Kraemer, Sebastian 59–60
Krampe, E. 56, 194–5

La Rossa, R. 54, 55, 58
Lamb, M. 48, 49, 52, 54
Lambert, L. 20, 22, 23, 30, 68, 77, 91, 116, 117, 137, 151, 159, 168
Langford, W. 133
Lewis, C. 11, 47, 48–9, 50, 52, 53, 54, 55, 56, 58, 133, 202, 204
Lightman, E. 105
Logan, J. 20, 22, 24, 42, 43, 68, 76, 126, 132, 133, 137, 138, 141, 152
Lupton, D. 48, 59, 133

MacKay, W. 57, 194, 195
Mander, R. 20, 68, 69, 91, 105, 153
March, K. 25, 31, 37, 38, 39, 41, 139, 161, 177, 181–2, 203–4
Marsiglio, W. 49, 53, 54, 57
Marwood, M. 181
Mason, J. 176, 179
Mason, M. 24, 36, 49
Massarik, F. 37, 73, 82, 84, 151, 197, 207
Masson, J. 204
May, K. 54, 55, 56, 58
McCarthy, P. 50
McCroy, R. 30
McHaffie, H. 120

McKee, L. 54
McMillan, R. 181
Mead, M. 56
Menard, B. 25, 26, 97
Mercer, R. 58
Millen, L. 117–19, 122, 135, 136
Miller, B. 54
Miller, J. 50, 51
Milligan, C. 50
Minton, C. 48, 52
Modell, J. 162, 177, 178, 180, 187, 193
Morrison, B. 197
Moss, P. 53
Mott, F. 52, 53
Mullender, A. 22, 34, 37, 43, 44, 45, 155, 166, 167, 169, 181, 191
Murphy, Cody 135, 162

Namerow, P. 65
National Association of Mental Health 29
Natural Parents Network 156
Natural Parents Support Group 20, 167
Newburn, M. 86
NORCAP 37
Nord, C. 50

O'Brien, M. 54
Orr, Deborah 205
Owens, D. 56

Pacheo, F. 39
Pannor, R. 23, 24, 25, 37, 39, 42, 73, 82, 84, 126, 135, 136, 153, 197, 207
Parkes, C. 117–18, 129
Pasley, K. 48, 52
Paterson, L. 30

Patti, P. 20, 25, 32–3, 34, 39, 42, 96, 147, 162, 163, 166, 195
Pavlovic, A. 204
Peterson, J. 50
Petrie, A. 21, 22
Phillips, Melanie 50
Pickford, R. 26, 203
Pill, C.J. 179
Platts, H. 23, 25, 105, 207
Pleck, J. 194
Popay, J. 53, 59
Post-Adoption Social Workers Group 37, 43, 178
Powell, S. 20, 22, 24, 64, 131
Princes Trust, The 50

Raynor, L. 68, 153
Rennell, T. 193
Richards, M. 54, 55, 58–9
Richman, J. 55, 56
Roberts, G. 120
Robertson, S. 59
Roll, S. 117–19, 122, 135, 136
Rolphe, J. 50
Roopnarine, J. 54
Rosenberg, E. 34, 108, 133, 147
Ross, J. 58
Rowe, J. 20, 55
Rutter, M. 59, 184
Ruxton, S. 26, 49, 50, 53
Ryan, J. 25, 32–3, 34, 39, 42, 96, 166
Ryan, M. 23, 204
Ryburn, M. 22, 23

Sachdev, P. 30, 37, 120, 194
Sargent, K. 57, 58
Sarre, S. 23, 25, 26, 47, 49, 51, 52, 58

Sawbridge, P. 17–18, 19, 20, 21, 23, 43, 55, 69, 73, 126, 133, 149, 161
Scarman, Mr. Justice 22, 23
Schechter, M. 25
Schlesinger, B. 105
Schwarz, 97
Scottish Office 42
Seabrook, S. 181
Seel, R. 55, 56
Shapiro, J. 53
Shaw, M. 24
Shawyer, J. 23
Silber, K. 37
Simpson, B. 50
Singh, D. 86
Skinner, C. 26, 49, 50, 51, 52, 53, 205
Sollid, D. 58
Soloman, Y. 133
Sorosky, A. 23, 126, 135, 136
Speak, S. 49, 50, 59, 192, 206
Speedlin, P. 37
Speirs, J. 30
Stimson, C. 26, 49, 50, 51, 52, 53, 205
Summers, Sue 205

Tabak, S. 37
Talk Adoption 20
Tamis–LeMonda, C. 48
Tanfer, K. 52, 53
Taylor, J. 41, 204, 207
Thoburn, J. 29–30, 32
Treboux, D. 184
Trinder, 166
Triseliotis, J. 20, 22, 23, 30, 33, 68, 77, 91, 116, 117, 137, 138, 151, 159, 161, 168, 178
Trotter, J. 204

Tugendhat, J. 19, 37, 39–40, 41, 55, 64
Turner, B. 193

van Keppel, M. 20, 21, 68, 105, 117, 135, 138, 160

Wadia-Ells, S. 22, 24
Walker, J. 50
Warin, J. 133
Warren, J. 20, 22, 24, 64, 131
Watson, K. 22, 25
Webb, E. 181
Weingarten, K. 55
Weinreb, M. 135, 162
Weiss, R. 123, 184, 185
Wells, S. 37, 42, 68, 138, 168
Welsh Office 21, 43
Williams, C. 22, 65
Williams, F. 52
Williams, J. 26, 49, 50, 51, 52, 53, 205
Williams, R. 59
Willmott, P. 94, 105
Wilson, E. 24
Winkler, R. 20, 21, 68, 105, 117, 135, 138, 160
Wolson, P. 57
Wynne-Edwards, K. 195

Yow, V. 66, 84

Zill, N. 50